Spiritual Energies

Awaken What's Within You With Everything You Need to Know About the 7 Spiritual Energies

Dawn Hazel

© Copyright 2022 - All rights reserved.

The content contained within this book may not be reproduced, duplicated or transmitted without direct written permission from the author or the publisher.

Under no circumstances will any blame or legal responsibility be held against the publisher, or author, for any damages, reparation, or monetary loss due to the information contained within this book, either directly or indirectly.

Legal Notice:

This book is copyright protected. It is only for personal use. You cannot amend, distribute, sell, use, quote or paraphrase any part, or the content within this book, without the consent of the author or publisher.

Disclaimer Notice:

Please note the information contained within this document is for educational and entertainment purposes only. All effort has been executed to present accurate, up to date, reliable, complete information. No warranties of any kind are declared or implied. Readers acknowledge that the author is not engaged in the rendering of legal, financial, medical or professional advice. The content within this book has been derived from various sources. Please consult a licensed professional before attempting any techniques outlined in this book.

By reading this document, the reader agrees that under no circumstances is the author responsible for any losses, direct or indirect, that are incurred as a result of the use of the information contained within this document, including, but not limited to, errors, omissions, or inaccuracies.

Table of Contents

INTRODUCTION 1
   FREEDOM TO EXPLORE YOUR SPIRITUALITY 2
      Sweep Your Fear Under the Rug 3
      Discovering the Energies That Surround You 4
   VENTURING OFF THE STRAIGHT AND NARROW PATH 5

CHAPTER 1: SPIRITUAL AWAKENING: THE JOURNEY TO EXPLORING YOUR SPIRITUALITY BEGINS RIGHT NOW 7
   UNDERSTANDING WHAT YOU CANNOT SEE 9
      Reassurance 9
      Defining Religion and Spirituality 10
   A CLOSER LOOK AT SPIRITUALITY 12
      Categorizing Spirituality 13
   EXPLORING YOUR SPIRITUALITY 15
      A Guide to Awaken Dormant or Non-existent Spirituality 16

CHAPTER 2: SPIRITUAL AWAKENING: ALIGNING YOUR SPIRITUALITY WITH A PLUCK HERE AND A JOSTLE THERE 21
   CHANGE YOUR AUTOPILOT LIFE 22
      Stop, Look, and Take Note 22
      Understanding Why Your Spiritual Universe Needs Attention 23
      Tried and Tested Tools to Strengthen Your Spirituality 24
   THE NEXT LEG OF THE ADVENTURE BEGINS HERE 29
      What Are Oracle Energies? 30
      The Center of Your Spiritual Universe 32
      All Aboard 33

CHAPTER 3: EARTH: THE CENTER OF YOUR SPIRITUAL UNIVERSE 35
   SYMBOLISM OF THE EARTH 36
      Representative of the Earth 37
      Tapping Into Different Spiritual Practices 39

CHAPTER 4: WATER: THE ELIXIR OF LIFE TO YOUR SPIRITUAL UNIVERSE 43
   THE SYMBOLISM OF WATER 44
      The Significance of Water in Different Parts of Our Lives 45
      Tapping Into Different Spiritual Practices 49

CHAPTER 5: FIRE: THE ETERNAL FLAME OF YOUR SPIRITUAL UNIVERSE 53

THE SYMBOLISM OF FIRE 55
The Power of Fire in Your Spiritual Universe 55
Tapping Into Different Spiritual Practices 60

CHAPTER 6: LOVE: THE UNIVERSAL LANGUAGE OF YOUR SPIRITUAL UNIVERSE 63

THE SYMBOLISM OF LOVE 65
Understanding the Power of Love in Your Spiritual Universe 66
Tapping Into Different Spiritual Practices 70

CHAPTER 7: SOUND: CREATIVE COMMUNICATION TO STRENGTHEN YOUR SPIRITUAL UNIVERSE 73

NAVIGATING YOUR SPIRITUAL COMMUNICATION CHANNELS 74
Listening to Your Spiritual Guides 76
Identifying Communication Channels 79
Tapping Into Different Spiritual Practices 81

CHAPTER 8: ENLIGHTENMENT: USING THE LIGHT OF YOUR SPIRITUAL UNIVERSE TO AWAKEN WHAT'S BEEN HIDDEN 83

ALLOW YOUR LIGHT TO SHINE 84
Tried and Tested Cleaning Methods and Tools 85
Tapping Into Different Spiritual Practices 89

CHAPTER 9: MIND: INTEGRATING THE LINE OF COMMUNICATION THAT SPEAKS DIRECTLY TO YOUR SPIRITUAL UNIVERSE 93

SETTING UP THE LINE OF COMMUNICATION 95
Opening the Doors to Your Mind Palace 96
Tapping Into Different Spiritual Practices 99

CONCLUSION 103

GRADUATION TIME 104
Slow and Steady 104
The Journey Ends Here 105

REFERENCES 107

IMAGE REFERENCES 112

Introduction

- Are you curious about what is going on in your mind, body, and soul?
- Are you curious about what is going on in the space that surrounds you?
- Are you experiencing feelings or emotions that cannot be explained?
- Are you struggling to pinpoint specific triggers that relate to what is happening in your life?
- Are your senses heightened when you are struggling with something related to life?
- Are you afraid to explore your spirituality?

I think that it is safe to assume that you have nodded *yes* in answer to some or all of these questions. You are not and will not be the first, second, or last person to be faced with these questions. I have found that many people get that "deer in the headlight look" the moment you mention something that would be considered taboo. That is when I feel as if I've been dumped into another dimension where I'm the Titanic and I am about to be rear-ended by an iceberg. Yes, this all sounds very dramatic, but bear with me because it will all make sense in a moment.

I don't like that people are afraid to be curious about what is going on around them. I have had people ask me why I would be writing books that "go against the Bible," or why I would be compromising my faith-based religion to make a 'quick' dollar. My answers are consistent—it is my mission to help everyone feel as if they are a part of this society called life. The only way I can achieve my mission is to show you, my loyal readers, that you are allowed to explore your spirituality. I am proud to offer you a safe space to learn about your spirituality without judgment and condemnation. The days where you have to hide behind closed doors and blackened windows are gone. You will not be struck by lightning, and you most definitely will not be burned at the stake for the curiosity displayed when exploring your spirituality.

Freedom to Explore Your Spirituality

Don't be afraid to be curious. Don't be afraid to explore your spirituality. God won't strike you down for being curious. God won't be angry with you. God loves everyone who walks around on this earth. God doesn't care about your gender, your ethnicity, whether you are wealthy or poor, or what you have done in your past, present, or future. God loved you before you were conceived, and he will love you when you leave this earth. It is time for everyone and their friends to stop condemning people for wandering off the straight and narrow path. The Bible is not meant to be taken literally, but it should be questioned and challenged. I would like to insert a disclaimer here by saying that these are my opinions, and what I believe may not align with what everyone else believes. I have spoken to many people while researching my books, and they have all uttered similar opinions and fears. It is time to pop the bubble and live your life the way you are meant to and not by being dictated to live in a certain way.

Sweep Your Fear Under the Rug

I have recently found that people are afraid to be curious. The world we live in is governed by people who find pleasure in filling our daily existence with fear. These fear-mongering individuals can come from television or radio broadcasts, printed media outlets on the Internet, or any of the various social media platforms. I like to refer to these people as armchair sleuths and gossipers who have nothing better to do with their time than spread doom and gloom. These are people who spend hours digging around on the Internet, reading blog posts and unverified news sources, and arriving at conclusions that missed the bus to Disney. The constant fighting, bickering, and tension within our communities, cities, or countries are based on fear and people's lack of understanding.

Who can and will ever forget the day the world came to a halt because of a global pandemic? We were thrust into a new world that had to be reformed and sculpted to accommodate you, me, and the rest of the world. I know of many people who plunged, headfirst, into religion to find answers about why this was happening. Many found solace in religion because of the uncertainty. More than many started reading their bibles by diving into the Book of Revelations because; hey, the world was coming to an end.

I discovered something else during this time, and that was that people became curious. They started experiencing unexplainable feelings and emotions which ranged from intense anger to heartbreak. There were also the many different signs that let people know that someone or something was trying to send them messages of peace, hope, and calm. People were telling me that they couldn't explain what or how they were feeling, but they had the urge to dig deeper to explore their feelings.

I realize that this is only a book that is filled with words. The words will give you a place where you can go to and get lost. A place where you can have a safe place to explore your spirituality. I wanted to create a place where you can understand what is going on in your spiritual universe. This safe haven and nonjudgmental space is coming to you hot off the heels of *Angel Numbers 1–9 Meaning: How To Understand the*

Divine Messages Angels Are Showing You for Twin Flames, Grief, Love, Change, Lost Loved Ones, Friends, and *Your Personalized Angel Guide: Introducing Archangels and Angels, and Understanding Who They Are and What Value They Add to Your Life.*

Discovering the Energies That Surround You

Have you read my book about angels and archangels? I highly recommend that you do, because I touch on relevant information that will lead you to believe that you are never alone. The angels possess energies that help you call for help, guidance, and protection. Guardian angels try to communicate with you by leaving you messages or giving you signs which include numbers, finding feathers, or lost objects miraculously appearing.

At any given time during your lifetime, you will encounter many types of people. Each type of person has an opinion that may not align with what you believe. I have found that the most common types of people are the skeptics, the nonbelievers, the believers, and the fundamentalists. I have crossed paths with all types of people, and I have had to endure a fair amount of condemnation because of my beliefs. "How can you call yourself a believer or a person of faith if you spend your time researching stuff that isn't in the Bible?" This is a statement I hear quite frequently.

My answer is quite simple in that you don't have to be submissive when it comes to faith-based religion. You have the right to ask questions. You are allowed to 'shop' around. You may be curious about what goes on in and around you. You don't have to give in to people who are trying to force their opinions on you. Not everything that happens is a coincidence. Not everything that happens is part of a vivid imagination. I want this book to help you peel back the layers and know what is going on behind every instance of your spiritual life.

Venturing off the Straight and Narrow Path

It is time to hop on board the Judgment-Free Fearless Train as we embark on this journey together. This ride is for everyone who wants to learn about the spiritual energies that form part of your daily lifestyle. No one is going to force you to sign any forms, and you will not be joining any cults. This journey, this judgment- and condemnation-free journey, is going to help you understand what you cannot explain.

The requirements for this journey include:
- an open mind
- beverages of choice
- sweet treats
- savory snacks
- a comfortable seat
- comfortable clothing
- your favorite fluffy socks

Call on your angels or say a prayer to help you navigate your way through this book. Let's leave the fear on the train tracks. This is your journey, and I want you to feel safe. This is a safe zone where you are allowed to walk around, open any doors you want, and dig around to your heart's content. You will not find any skeletons on this journey and no one will taunt you with their bony fingers. It is time for your conductor—that will be me—to crank up the power on this train. Sit back and enjoy your journey with me. Let's get this spiritual journey started.

Chapter 1:

Spiritual Awakening: The Journey to Exploring Your Spirituality Begins Right Now

We are more alike than you would care to admit. You may be shaking your head in disagreement. You may be thinking that I don't know what I'm talking about. You may be angry because I dare to utter that we are alike. You may even be nodding in agreement that we might be called two peas in a pod.

This is not a competition to see who is better at this, that, and the other. No one is going to rate you for your mistakes or failures. Everyone is so eager to be one up on the next person, that you forget who or where you are. I am not sitting on a platform looking down at you. I am sitting where you are, and I'm seeing the views you are. Our locations might vary, but we all see hurt, anger, pain, love, happiness, and a myriad of different emotions. We are not involved in a power struggle for whatever top spot is calling your name.

I am not a minister or a pastor, nor am I a priestess. I am a normal human being—as normal as one can be, I guess. I have my faults and I am not perfect. I embrace my imperfections with a massive bear hug. I am religious and I am spiritual—and I am so very curious, which is why I am pouring my abundance of energies into words. I want to share what is going on in my head. I want you to know that it is okay to challenge your faith.

I have previously mentioned that you will always be loved by God, because He created you. He is the only one that knows how many hairs you have on your head. He was even so creative that He gave you a set of fingerprints that identify you. Think about it for a moment; in a world that houses over seven billion people, no one else has your fingerprints. God knows what you are going to think about before the thought pops into your mind. He knows what you're going to be doing before you do it. You can't hide from God, just like Eve couldn't hide when she had eaten the forbidden fruit.

Human beings are curious by nature. We are never satisfied with an answer that offers no explanations. We may say that we are happy with the outcome of a specific scenario, when in truth we want to dig a little deeper until we find what we are looking for. God knows all of this because he knows us. He allows us to explore our curiosity. He gives you enough to satisfy your curiosity. What you do with the information you have gathered is up to you. And again, you may not be happy with what you have gathered, and therefore you continue digging. God never gives you more than you can handle.

Understanding What You Cannot See

I have always put religion and spirituality in the same category. I believed that I was pretty knowledgeable, until I realized that religion and spirituality are two different topics. I spoke to a lot of people during the research phase of my books. I wanted to understand what others were saying, and very quickly I learned that not everyone will be pleased with the results. I continued with my research, though, because I wanted to get everyone's perspective. One thing I learned was that no one is the same and everyone has their own interpretation about what the relationship between religion and spirituality entails. I became intrigued and, yes, curious—very curious.

I have had people tell me that what I am doing is interfering with God's plans. I was told that I would be judged by God. You can't intertwine the two topics, because you are going against the Bible. I have been seeing and hearing a whole lot of "you can't," "you will," or "you are," since I started writing my books. I am amazed that so many people have become knowledgeable on the subjects of religion and spirituality—and I understand that everyone will have an opinion, but who gives anyone the right to chastise us for our beliefs? I have developed a thick skin over the last couple of years, and am protected against the negativity that is thrown my way. I will not allow any of these negative energies to seep into my mind, body, and soul. I want everyone who reads this to know that you, too, can cloak yourself in anti-negativity gear.

Reassurance

I would like us to take a look at the differences between religion and spirituality. This is not going to be a section about making you choose one over the other, but rather I want you to remember that you have a choice: you can choose to be both religious and spiritual, or you can choose to be one or the other. Whatever option you choose is between you and your deity of choice. I want to equip you with a voice so that you can stand up against those who want to push you into a box. The sand is running out on those who want to force you to think, believe, and behave like them.

I want to reinforce, in case you missed it before, that you are your own person. What that means is that you have the freedom to explore and challenge your beliefs, faith, religion, and spirituality. You may have noticed that I am passionate about equipping everyone with freedom. I want you to have the freedom to make decisions that will help you find your place in this crazy world we find ourselves in. I have shared my visions for this book with my editor and my publisher so that we are all on the same page. My books are not going to suppress you, nor will they force you to choose. We want you to be happy because your happiness is important to your spirituality.

Defining Religion and Spirituality

I want to give you all the information you will need to equip your toolbox as we progress through this chapter, as well as the rest of this book. I will reiterate that not everyone will be on the same wavelength or page as you, and this is perfectly normal. You are free to form your own opinions, even though they may not align with what others believe. This book is about you and your journey, and therefore does not include the opinions of your neighbors, your best friends, or your family.

I previously mentioned that I had believed that religion and spirituality were the same. I am one of those who believes that religion and spirituality are intertwined, even though they have different definitions. I am strongly aware that I may be in the minority with my beliefs, but in all honesty, this is what gets me through a very long and busy day at work. I like to imagine that my beliefs ensure that I have the best of both worlds. I see both sides of this as a blessing because my mind, body, and soul are at peace.

Religion

The Merriam-Webster online dictionary defines religion as being part of a personal system or organization that advocates faith-based views, beliefs, and practices. The definition of religion includes serving God in worship and prayer as well (Merriam-Webster, 2019d). You don't need a dictionary to read between the lines to fill in some gaps relating to how you perceive religion to be. Everyone, at some stage during their lifetime, has attended Sunday school or participated in some form of religious study.

My take on religion includes upholding The Ten Commandments and living in faith that God is our protector. He sacrificed His Son, Jesus Christ, to atone for our trespasses. His body was broken so that we may be forgiven for all eternity. I have had people ask me why I would believe in someone or something where pain, suffering, hatred, anger, or destruction was permitted. I honestly wish I had an answer to give to these people, but I don't. Saying that I can feel it in my gut is not going to be a satisfactory answer. I do know for sure that I am at peace with God's plans for my future. I know and understand that people are angry, especially when senseless acts of violence or unnecessary illnesses claim the lives of innocent people. The only advice I can give, which works for me, is to believe that everything happens the way it is meant to.

Spirituality

Spirituality doesn't force you to be part of any particular faith-based organization. We know that religion is based on the words, laws, and affirmations stated in the Bible. Spirituality is about what is going on in your mind, body, and soul. No one can force you to be spiritual or participate in activities relating to spirituality. No one can prevent you from following your beliefs. Spirituality is a private affair that affects your mind, body, and soul. Your spirituality is tailored to fit you, and no two people will have the same experiences.

Your spiritual beliefs will change over time, and this is a normal occurrence. It may be that what you once believed in has frizzled away and become redundant, or it may just be that your spiritual goals have become stronger. It could also be that you have control over what happens in your life. I love knowing that I can either feed my curiosity or weed out old spiritual beliefs with the intention of growing in my spirituality; I love knowing that I have options that are mine; and I love the idea of holding onto my beliefs and not sharing them because others may not understand my motives.

A Closer Look at Spirituality

The previous section showed you the difference between religion and spirituality. I explained how the two may look, sound, and act in similar ways—but yet they are different. The difference may be ever so slight or it may be huge; you won't know until you put your spirituality to the test. I have also explained that no two people will have the same spiritual beliefs or experiences. It is your choice about how you want to adopt or approach spiritual affairs—you want to grow your spirituality based on your needs.

I was introduced to the following analogy by someone I spoke with while doing research for my book about the seven spiritual energies. I had to start somewhere, and you know it—learning about spirituality was the first station I stopped at on our journey. The lady I spoke with told me that spirituality is similar to the sourdough bread starter which is cultivated, grown, and nurtured on your kitchen counter:

1. Someone will share a bit of their sourdough starter (or you start from scratch).
2. You have to discard some of the starter to make room to grow.
3. You then get to feed your starter.
4. You repeat the previous two steps until your starter is bubbling, rising, and looking healthy.
5. At this point, you may want to repeat steps one and two twice a day.
6. Eventually, you are in a position where your starter is ready to be used to bake that perfect sourdough bread.
7. You can share the fruits of your starter and spread the love.

Can you imagine receiving the starter from someone and immediately using what you have to bake your bread? You will not have that perfectly formed, pillowy fluffy, and delicious bread you had dreamed about. Why not? Because you were impatient and didn't treat your starter with the respect it needed. This is what building your spirituality is like. You need to practice caution and test the waters.

I know that we are quick to want to follow what our idols are doing; but the truth is that we don't know what they are telling us to incorporate into our lives. I don't know about you, but I don't like it when someone comes to me and tells me that I should do this, that, and the other. They will proceed to tell me that it is something life-changing, and that I will never look back once I align my beliefs with them. I'm so sorry to pop your bubble, but I'm not going to adopt something that I haven't put to the test. Spoiler alert—I will never force my readers to believe in something because I said so! The way it works is that I give you the information and you get to go and test it out; and once you have done what is needed, you can come back and tell me about your experience. Do we have a deal? Good!

Categorizing Spirituality

Spirituality comes in all shapes and sizes. It is not a one-size-fits-all type of belief system. Your spiritual experience is unique to you and your circumstances. You could share your experience with others, but no one else will understand the effect it has on you. I am a curious person and I want my readers to have as much information as possible. You would be correct in assuming that I went digging for information. I stumbled across different types of spiritualities that had me sit up and take notice.

Firstly, I believe that the different categories are an indication of where you could potentially find yourself on the spiritual hierarchy. Secondly, and most importantly, I believe that this part of the chapter is going to pave the way forward for the duration of our journey together. This book is about discovering the spiritual energies that form part of your spiritual universe. These energies surround us, as well as form part of our minds, bodies, and souls. This is where the naysayers will dive in and have their opinions—but as I have stated, you don't need to be intimidated by anyone or anything. You are not going to sign up for anything and you won't be brainwashed. Once again, all I am asking of you is to have an open mind so that you can tame that little feather that is tickling your curiosity.

Let's start this little side trip with a look at the different types of spiritualities. You may find that one or more of these categories accurately define where you are in your spiritual journey. It always helps to have an example or an idea to look back on and reach your *aha* moment when the pieces of the puzzle fall into place.

Mind and Thought

You may be the thinker. You are the type of person that jumps into a situation without finding out all the facts. You ask many questions while trying to understand what you are experiencing. You may be the type of person that will dry out the resources and still want to find more information. You won't leave any stone unturned during your quest to understand your spirituality.

Supernatural Intuition

No, this is not about Sam and Dean Winchester from the television series *Supernatural*. This category aligns with religion and people's perception of what spirituality is. You are a believer in what is going on and you live your life according to your religious upbringing. You may be from any one of the thousands of faith-based religions. You may be led by your conscience and the need to always do what is right. Your spirituality is guiding you along that smooth pathway and will assist you when you stumble. You are acutely aware that everything in your life happens as it is meant to, regardless of whether it is good or bad. I previously mentioned that God allows things to happen because it is part of our destinies on this earth.

The Helping Hand

This type of spirituality is very special, but it may also present you with some problems. If this is one of your categories, I am going to issue you a little warning—one that you may have encountered in the past, but going forward, you can protect yourself against. People who are blessed with a caring and helpful spirit are often taken advantage of. I say this out of experience, because I know many people who have been at the receiving end. It becomes difficult to differentiate between the people who genuinely need assistance and those who just want to take all the time. It is okay to say *no* to those who continue to come back for more. You get to make the rules.

Exploring Your Spirituality

I know how difficult it is to have something embedded in your soul that sets you apart from others. I shared some of the most common types of spiritualities in the previous section; and I didn't want to overwhelm you with the information, because I am pretty sure that your senses are in overdrive right now. You are trying to put a name on your spiritual gift. The list is endless, and can include something as simple as sharing the love you have with those who don't have that luxury. You could be an empath or have the gift of discernment, where you feel people's emotions. I spoke to someone who told me that when they heard that the legendary *Golden Girl*, Betty White, had passed away just 17 days before her 100th birthday, they said that they broke down and sobbed for someone they had never met. They said that they experienced the same emotions when the news broke announcing the death of the *Full House* and *Fuller House* actor and comedian, Bob Saget. I asked them to describe what they were feeling and they responded that it felt like climbing into a bathtub full of water and watching the water spill all over the floor.

I do understand that not everyone has discovered, or is in tune with, their spirituality. This doesn't mean that they are not spiritual, though. Everyone who lives on this earth is spiritual in their own way. It is not up to you or me to say anything different. Adopt the spirituality of not condemning others for their beliefs or lack thereof. See everyone as an equal. Now, I'm not saying that you should like everyone. There may be some nerve end graters that cross our paths multiple times a day, and the best we can do is greet them with a smile. You don't know what the other person is going through, because they are reserved or afraid to speak up.

Not everyone understands the meaning of spirituality and how it affects their lives, so I thought it would be an excellent idea to put together a little guide on how to explore your spirituality. I'm not saying that you need to reevaluate where you are on your spiritual journey, but everyone could benefit from a refresher. This little guide will also be a way in which you can help someone else who you may believe is struggling to understand their spiritual light. May I add that this section could be left open on your desk at work, on your coffee table, or in the bathroom. If you are reading this as a digital version, you may want to leave your Kindle, eReader, laptop, or iPad open when you have guests around. Oh, we *know* that people are curious when they see something that they believe is private. Don't go shaking your head either, because I know that you know you do it when you go visiting, too.

A Guide to Awaken Dormant or Non-existent Spirituality

We have ascertained that not everyone will be at a level that is consistent with what you are experiencing. Some people may have their spirituality hidden behind locked doors, and others may be ignoring the glaringly obvious signs. This little guide is meant to help you explore what you have hidden or ignored. I am giving everyone reading this section a master key to unlock the door to their spiritual soul. You don't have to do anything once you've opened that door—you will still be the same person you were before you read this section. I'm not going to change you or change the course of your life journey.

I am and will be giving you a glimpse of what you already have in your soul. I am going to shine my torch on what you have hidden away. I am going to attempt to help you understand that you are a spiritual person. I want you to learn how to embrace your gifts. I want you to feel comfortable with your newfound spirituality that will be unleashed or rekindled. Remember that this is your safe space, and no one can hurt you in this book. The words you are reading are nonjudgmental, and no one will be reaching through the pages to punch you for the decisions you make.

Be Respectful at All Times

A little respect goes a long way. The question of where spirituality originated is not based on some idea that Joe woke up with two or three years ago. Spirituality has been around since before humans found their way to earth. The only epiphany Joe woke up with was when his spirituality was activated. This normally occurs when something in his subconscious is triggered. Please remember that not everyone will have the same beliefs as you, and not everyone has a religious background. These are personal choices that need to be respected. Always be conscientious of everyone's feelings and situations. You don't know how or why their spiritual door has not been revealed to them.

This Is Your Journey

You cannot—and should not—dictate someone else's spiritual journey for them. Everyone embarks on a unique spiritual journey when the time is right for them. You shouldn't use fast passes to skip through the fundamental learning curves. You don't have a time limit in which to complete your journey. This spiritual journey is not about your spouse, your partner, or the man on the street—and it is yours to navigate as you see fit. Listen to what your heart is telling you. You will feel an unfamiliar *knock, knock* in your soul—and you should then begin to feel your heart doing a jiggle in your chest cavity. What happens after that is acceptance, understanding, and action. Remember that this is your journey and no one has permission to tell you how it should be navigated.

Help Is Closer Than You Think

The help I am alluding to here is not the *pick up the phone to call your friend who lives three states away* kind of help. The type of help I am referring to is not going to cost you a dime, nor will you be expected to exchange any favors. When you feel that you are struggling with your spirituality, you can call out to your deity of choice or your guardian angels. Everyone is waiting for you to send out your cry for help. If you are anything like me, I know that you don't want to burden anyone with your questions, let alone ask for help. I have had to learn the hard way that our spiritual guides are waiting for us to ask them for help. Ask for courage if you are afraid. Ask for guidance when you are uncertain. Ask for a smile when you are feeling sad. Ask for your heart to be accepting when you are struggling. Friends, you only need to think about the word 'help' for your guides to flood you with whatever you need. You don't need to be the hero that carries all the baggage.

When the Time Is Right

Not many people like to practice the sport of patience. Yes, I did say it's a sport because, in reality, we don't want to wait. I can almost blame it on the fast-paced world we live in where everything needs to be done in the blink of an eye. I do believe that the world slowed down in 2020 when lockdown restrictions were put in place because of the global pandemic. People took that time to find themselves, with many turning to religion or tapping into their spirituality. A lot of questions, prayers, and requests for assistance were asked from all spiritual-related parties. I remember the frustration that friends and family experienced whenever they diligently prayed or called on their angels. Their cries or pleas for help seemed to go unanswered. The truth is that it would seem that way because of being impatient. Everything, whether it be obstacles you are facing or answers to questions asked, happens when the time is right. I learned that time stands still in the spiritual universe. A month on earth is only a second to our spiritual guides. Practice patience and have a little faith that your answer will come to you when the time is right.

Why Wait for Tomorrow?

I find it interesting that people will wait for the New Year to make resolutions, that they will start their diet on a Monday, or that they will quit smoking at the beginning of a new month. Why does everything need to be scheduled? Is it because you need to be prepared for the changes that will take effect? I don't think that anyone has any logical explanation for why everything needs to be scheduled. And now I am going to tell you to stop procrastinating. Benjamin Franklin said something that could have been written for this section, and that is, *"don't put off until tomorrow what you can do today."*

Everyone has something special and unique about what is going on in their souls. Some people are masters at keeping their souls blocked off from others for fear of being taken advantage of. Others walk around allowing their souls to shine for everyone to see. It doesn't matter which type of person you are—but I want you to know that you are special. You have a gift that is waiting to be unleashed into this crazy world. You may believe that you are an insignificant person among a population of over seven billion. Do you want to know something special, though? There is only *one* you. How many people do you think you have touched in the last week? None, you say? One? Three? I would venture to say that you have touched an infinite number of people.

One smile or act of kindness—which you may not have even noticed—touched someone's heart. You didn't notice the troubled teen who opened the door for you at the dentist. Your smile and "thank you" touched their heart when they needed it the most. They then went out and spread that love or smile, and it spread like wildfire. Why? Because your gentle, grateful, and kind spirit prompted you to smile, and say two little magic words. Don't wait until tomorrow to explore your spirituality. Someone needs you to share your gift with them today.

Chapter 2:

Spiritual Awakening: Aligning Your Spirituality With A Pluck Here and a Jostle There

Please don't let the title of this section scare you as there will be no plucking. There may be some jostling, but I promise to keep the shake-up to a minimum. Until now, you have explored your spirituality. You have learned that whatever gifts you have hiding in your spiritual closet are meant to be shared. The time has finally arrived for you to use that master key I issued you with. You are going to unlock your spiritual door, and unleash your beautiful mind, body, and soul.

This section of the book is going to be a tool kit for what you can do to pluck your spiritual gifts out of your closet. You will learn how to keep your gifts clean and shiny, but don't fret too much if you should experience some dust or grime in the future. This handy tool kit is going to show you how to manage, polish, and realign your spirituality in pretty easy-to-understand ways. The best part about this tool kit is that you have heard of these activities. You most probably have even practiced or participated in some of them. Some may also be too far outside of your comfort zone to try, or you have been afraid to be curious.

This tool kit is for everyone who is on their spiritual journey. You are free to utilize any or all of the examples given. This spiritual universe is yours where you can build a space that you know no one can destroy. I want you to know that this tool kit has no restrictions. You can accomplish anything you put your mind to, because this is your special place. Your spiritual universe is your escape room and you can spend time using your tool kit to strengthen your soul.

Change Your Autopilot Life

Have you ever done something without realizing that it may be beneficial to your health and well-being? I do believe I can answer this for the majority of my readers by saying—no. We tend to go through life on autopilot. It has to do with the fast-paced world we live in and the need to do everything in the blink of an eye. Everything becomes a blur, and you forget to put thought into what you are doing. I would like to give you a little task. Feel free to change the scene to suit your situation. I do ask that you participate so that you have an idea of what you may be experiencing. I'm not going to climb into your mind or suggest anything—I merely want you to understand what you are doing when you go through life in a blur.

Stop, Look, and Take Note

Take a couple of deep breaths. Breathe in through your nose and exhale through your mouth. This exercise should calm your heart that is thumping against your rib cage. Now imagine that you are at the mall. You are surrounded by people who have one goal in mind, and that is to get in and grab what they need, and then get out. The majority of the people are looking down at their smartphones while they go from store to store. People are walking into each other, and you can see the anger on the faces of those who notice others staring at their phones. How dare they not look where they are walking?

You see yourself hustling to get to Bath & Body Works to buy a birthday gift for your mother. You are zigzagging through crowds of people to get there before the store closes. You make it in the nick of time, and grab whatever you think your mother will like. You are not giving the gift any thought. You pay and head out, and you were in and out of the store in 10 minutes. You zigzag your way through the crowds to get to your car because you have to go to your mother's birthday dinner. You get to your car and realize that not only do you have a flat tire, but someone dented the driver's door. You look around for a note on your windshield, but there is nothing. This leaves you feeling defeated, as if the world and its elements are against you.

Understanding Why Your Spiritual Universe Needs Attention

I know people who have been in similar situations as depicted above. We are so quick to point the finger and lay the blame on everyone else, and we are invisible to the blame we pass on. Oh, for sure that flat tire was a personal attack directed at you, because *no one* else ever gets flat tires. The dent in the door was done with malicious intent. You are so absorbed in negative thoughts that you don't want to recognize what these signs are trying to tell you.

I'm going to tell you to stop what you're doing. You need to take a step back and add up all the signs. You were rushing through the mall to get to the store before it closed. You chose a gift that you just grabbed without thinking: "Hey, will Mom like this?" You rushed to get out of the mall so that you could get ready for a dinner party. You get to your car and find out that you not only have a flat tire, but a massive dent in the driver's side as well. Are you seeing what I'm seeing? Surely these are signs from your spiritual universe. What are they trying to tell you? Let's take a look:

- Maybe you should slow down.
- Maybe you should take some time to think about a gift.
- The flat tire could be an indication that you are not meant to be driving at that time.
- The dent could be part of the plan to slow you down.

And you say that the world and its elements are against you? No, no one is against you. You are ignoring the signs that are in front of you. That is why I am going to fill up your tool kit, in addition to helping you do a good spit and polish job on your tools.

Tried and Tested Tools to Strengthen Your Spirituality

You are edging closer to discovering what spiritual energies are and what they can mean for your spiritual well-being. I am going to equip your tool kit with helpful tools. You are going to learn how to build, furnish, and take care of your spiritual universe. I want to ensure that you have a starter kit of everything you need to grow your spirituality, or to rekindle the flame that has been snuffed out. The tool kit that I will be sharing with you can be added to, items can be removed, or you can create tools that work for you. Remember, this is your journey and *you* are the tour operator. Make good choices and spread your spiritual gifts with everyone you meet along your journey.

Journaling

This has to be one of my favorite tools. I had to add it at the top of the list, because writing has helped me reach an audience that looks for peace, calm, and serenity in words. I had someone tell me that they have hundreds of notebooks full of short stories, novels, and journal entries. Their collection dates back to the 1980s. I asked why they hadn't turned their writing into books to share with the world and they laughed at me. They said that their words were not meant to be read by anyone other than themselves. They saw my frown of confusion, and went on to explain that they had turned to writing to help them with some issues relating to familial bullying and loneliness.

Journaling is a way to express your feelings. You will begin to feel better once the feelings have been transferred from your mind to the paper. In essence, you are getting all the negative thoughts out of your mind. This is something you may want to do multiple times a day, because you definitely don't want the toxic negativity to suppress your spiritual energy. You can share your journals with people if you believe that they need help, or you could have a "negative send-off" party. Oh, I feel that frown. A negative send-off party is where you light a fire in your firepit and you toss in your journal. You can say words of affirmation, you can pray, you can meditate, you can speak to your angels, or anything else you want to as you watch the negative energy go up in smoke. Do not send the journal off with negative energy, because you want to fill the universe with positivity. Yes, this is one of the most satisfying experiences I have ever participated in—and which I continue to do.

Seeking Forgiveness

- Have you ever said something hurtful to someone in the heat of the moment?
- Have you ever purposely hurt someone because you believe that they did something out of spite?
- Have you ever been hurt by someone who you loved and trusted with your life?
- Have you ever wished harm on someone because you were so angry with them?
- Has anyone ever taken something from you that you have never forgotten about?
- Has anyone ever said something to you that has been burned into your mind?

If you have answered *yes* to any of these questions, then I am going to tell you that you need to let go and forgive. You can't expect your spirit to be free if you are not letting go of the stifling darkness. You may not realize it, but the darkness and negativity that you are saving (for whatever reason) are going to cause a blockage in your spiritual universe. It is going to suppress you as a person, which will negatively affect your spirituality.

You need to understand that whatever you are holding onto will always be with you. It is a battle only you will understand. The anger, hatred, and negativity will follow you to the grave because you have allowed it to consume you in life. I know what it is like to carry around old and tattered luggage that is useless. All it is doing is dragging you down. Someone shared their story about forgiveness with me, and I knew that I had to share it with you in order to show you what can happen if you forgive.

The person I am referencing is a middle-aged lady who lost her mother to a heart attack after she had been verbally and mentally attacked by her grandmother. The lady, who is both religious and spiritual, carried around a lot of anger because of what her grandmother had done. Her mother pleaded with her not to be angry and blame her grandmother for hurting her with venomous words. She said that she wouldn't and had believed that she had forgiven her grandmother. Over the course of eight years, the lady did her best to keep the promise she'd made to her mother. The world went into lockdown at the beginning of 2020, and people were not allowed to visit their family members in care facilities. The lady went to see her grandmother, and when she hugged her, she knew in her heart that it would be the last time she would ever see her alive again. It was then, standing under an umbrella of oak leaves, that she asked for forgiveness for the feelings she had been holding onto. Six months after letting go of the old baggage, her grandmother left this earth with a smile on her face. Her smile had been lost for so many years, but it had returned as she started her new journey because she knew that she had been forgiven.

Forgiveness is healing for the soul. It is an excellent feng shui tool. Reach out to those you hurt and ask them for forgiveness. Reach out to those who have hurt you and let them know that you forgive them. You can always forgive, but you will always remember. What you remember is a carbon copy of what happened, but the original has been destroyed and cannot come back to haunt you. Let go and watch as your spirit soars because it is free.

Visiting Places That Speak to Your Soul

Do you have a favorite place that could be defined as the center of your universe? You may not agree with me, but I do believe that everyone has a special place like that. You can have more than one special place that you feel connected to. Many people have said that their special place is going to the beach at sunset. They say that there is something special about watching the ocean seem to absorb the sun as it goes down. Some have said that they feel close to their deities, and others have said that they engage in two-way conversations with their spiritual guides. Many have indicated that their go-to place is the mountains. They believe that nothing is more relaxing than watching the sun being slowly pushed up above the mountaintops.

Everyone has a place that screams peace and tranquility. It doesn't matter who you are or where you live, but you need to find a place where you can be at peace with yourself. Your very own sacred place where you can connect with your spiritual universe. You need to find that place where you can clear your soul of the unnecessary baggage you carry with you. I will attempt to give you a few ideas of where you could find a place where you could tap into your spiritual universe. These ideas may trigger some memories you have blocked or forgotten as you went through various stages of your life:

- enjoying a picnic at the park
- strolling down tree-lined avenues or hiking in the forests
- fishing at the local river, stream, or lake
- sitting between the shelves of books at the local library
- visiting the museum
- walking through a gallery
- visiting temples or churches
- sitting at the wall of remembrance at your local cemetery
- creating a garden at your home
- hiding out in the bathroom for privacy

The ideas and options are never-ending. You don't have to worry about choosing the right or wrong place. Your spiritual universe will guide you to your special place. Always be attentive to your senses.

Conversations With the Universe

You may be frowning as you contemplate where I am going with the heading of this section. This is where the naysayers will come with their pitchforks and burning stakes to tell you that what you are doing is wrong and goes against everything that is religion-based. How can you have a conversation with the universe? What does it entail? Why can't you just spend your time praying and asking God to guide you?

The world we live in has evolved, and what our forefathers believed in 10, 20, 30, or 80 years ago no longer exists. No one could have foreseen that the world would be standing at over seven billion people, or that there would be thousands of different religions or religious denominations. No one is asking you to change your beliefs to align with the beginning of time. No one is going to break your spirit because you do not believe what others believe. Oh, they can try—and they will—but you don't have to bow to their demands because you have a choice.

History books have indicated that the practice of meditation originated in India more than a thousand years ago (Chow, 2021). It has been adapted over time so that people from all walks of life can be part of this ritual. I have seen many religions adopt meditation as part of their daily lives. It doesn't matter if you are Hindu, Muslim, Islam, Christian, or atheist. Meditation is an excellent tool to help you find your journey to spiritual peace and happiness. With my tongue in my cheek, I would say that everyone needs someone to talk to who doesn't talk back, or argue with them. Find a quiet place in your home, garden, office, or car, and talk to the universe. Put your heart out there. Before you know it, you will start noticing a shift in your spiritual balance as the blockages start moving.

More Examples of Tools

The list of tools to align your spirituality is long. This is a subject I am passionate about, because I know what it is like to feel out of sorts with my spiritual universe. I have had people share their stories about why they need to utilize tools to help center or ground their spirituality. I have spoken to empaths who have said that without the spiritual alignment tools, they would be locked in an asylum because they feel and absorb the sadness, anger, and pain of those who are connected to them. For the sake of your spiritual universe and spiritual energies, take care of your gifts by respecting them and caring for them the way you care for your children or pets.

1. Practice movement by dancing, running, yoga, pilates, or cardio exercises, including working in the garden and sweeping, mopping, or vacuuming your home.
2. You don't always have to be perfect at everything, so don't beat yourself up if you don't reach a goal or you disappoint someone—tomorrow is another day.
3. You don't have to be a spiritualist hero who needs to do everything; reach out for help by visiting forums, social media groups, or members of your community for support.
4. Practice self-care and take time to put yourself first and everyone else second—guilt-free rules apply.
5. You could read your deck of oracle cards, or visit a trusted spiritual reader to enlighten and uplift you with their reading—this is a topic we will be looking into later in the book.

The Next Leg of the Adventure Begins Here

Chapters 1 and 2 have been packed with information to help you along on your spiritual journey. I have filled your tool kit with many useful tips that can be modified to suit your requirements. You don't have to be afraid to use what you have learned. The knowledge that you have already gained will be expanded upon as this journey continues. You will experience many emotions during your journey such as anger, frustration, or the feeling of being helpless—which is normal. You can use your tools to clear those blockages or negative energies.

I think, no—I am confident that you are ready for the next leg of your journey. The first two chapters were all about equipping you with the tools needed to prepare your mind, body, and soul for this journey. You know that feeling you have in the pit of your stomach? You know... that feeling you can't quite put your finger on? Yes, that one! You never have a name for it, but your intuition (or your gut feeling) may have picked up on it. The next seven chapters are going to revolve around identifying seven spiritual energies that are present in your spiritual universe.

I realize that I could have jumped right in and informed you about the spiritual energies in your spiritual universe, but I know that you would have more questions and be more confused than before you started on this journey. I did a lot of research before I started writing this book. I was left gripping my hair in my hands because all my research led me to established authors on this topic. I wanted something unique, and I believe that I may have achieved that goal. I needed to know what I wanted before I could share it with you. I had to ease into the topic of spiritual energies because I didn't want to overwhelm you or make you feel as if you are compromising your beliefs. I believe that you are ready for that next step. You have learned to awaken and align your spirituality with the tools, tips, and tricks I have provided. I needed to show you everything before we could continue on the mystical trip to discover the spiritual energies and what value they could add to your spiritual universe.

What Are Oracle Energies?

If you are anything like me, curious and ready to find fault with anything you read, then you have most probably searched Google for information about "oracle energy." The first entry to pop up on your screen is most likely one that will refer you to a power company, and the rest of the entries will echo that of the first one. Yes, I have been down that energy hole, and I endured more frustration than I can put into words. Internet searches become interesting when you add certain keywords, and before you know it, you have a smidgen of information that leads you all around the globe in 10 clicks.

It was important to start my adventure into the spiritual universe with oracle energies, but you may notice that the further we advance through the book, I change the dynamics and focus on spiritual energies. Oracle energy practitioners will become part of the chapters under the headings of *Tapping Into Different Spiritual Practices*. I wanted to put together an all-in-one resource guide that features an original interpretation of what the various oracle energies mean to your life.

I have done a lot of research, and I have read many books by various authors regarding this subject. As of yet, I have not found anything that grabbed my attention enough to satisfy my curiosity. That was when I decided that I was going to use what I have learned to present you with an easy-to-understand interpretation. My biggest wish is that you will use the information to navigate your way through your spiritual universe—a place that you have created to fit your needs and circumstances.

I turned to the Merriam-Webster online dictionary for assistance in hopes of giving you a clear definition of what "oracle energy" is. I concluded that each word has its own definition, and that they don't appear to be intertwined. Let's have a look at the definitions to see if we can have a clearer understanding.

Oracle Meaning

According to Merriam-Webster, an oracle is referred to as a spiritual person who is a vessel for telling people what they see in their future. Some people may think of an oracle as a practicing fortune-teller who shares their opinions of what they see in your cards, palms, or stars. Others may think of an oracle as someone who sees into your soul, and prophesizes what they believe they see. The belief is also held that God chooses religious people, members of the cloth, or deeply spiritual individuals to share His word or visions with others (Merriam-Webster, 2019c).

We know that this topic is one huge prickly pear. This is why people who don't understand or take the time to research topics will have negative input. It is for this exact reason that I wanted to write this book to show everyone that not everything has to be 'evil' or 'impure.' It doesn't matter which deity you believe in, or which religion you follow—you have the choice to follow your beliefs. You know that there is nothing wrong with being curious.

Energy Meaning

I know that I don't have to give you a description of what energy is, because we all took science during our schooling years. Most people don't realize that they use energy every day. We consume carbohydrates, which our bodies break down into sugar. The sugar we consume is then turned into energy that is transported through our bodies to reach various organs and cells (Dowshen, 2022).

This book doesn't require you to understand all the different types of energies and what they represent. The Merriam-Webster dictionary gives various definitions based on the different categories, and I wanted to give you the definition that closely resembles the subject at hand which relates to our spirituality. Your mind, body, and soul are like a generator that feeds off both positive and negative vibes or energies. What this means is that we absorb these different types of energies and they, in turn, fuel our spirits which are then released. Some people will direct their spiritual energy positively and calmly. Others may release their negative energies in the form of anger (Merriam-Webster, 2019a).

The Center of Your Spiritual Universe

This journey is all about you. No one can tell how you should or shouldn't be feeling. You are the host and caretaker of your mind, body, and soul. You decide the fate of what you want to do with your spirituality. I feel strongly that everyone who is of an able mind, body, and age have the choice to do what is best for them. It is very common for strangers to give you the evil eye when they see you consuming something that could be potentially harmful to your health. It is easy to point fingers and pass judgment, but in reality, they don't see you every day. Why should it matter to a stranger if you're carrying around a couple of extra pounds? Why should it matter to your sibling if you've decided to dye your hair pink? Why should it matter to anyone what you do?

I believe that people should stop pointing fingers of discrimination at others. Instead, they should focus on themselves, their families, their health, and live their lives according to their standards. There is enough hatred and anger across the globe to fuel a spaceship. The time has come to replace those negative energies with positive lights. A smile, a wave, or a friendly word is what people need. This journey is going to be a personalized and practical guide to teach you how to turn on and keep your spiritual light burning. You will also learn how to share and touch those you meet with your spiritual light.

Your spiritual universe is a sacred place where your mind, body, and soul reside. This special place is where you can go to find yourself during difficult situations or circumstances. This is your escape room, away from the hustle and bustle of real life. Use the tools in your tool kit to re-energize yourself. Call on your angels for guidance. Practice meditation to help you focus. You do what you need to do to awaken, reenergize, or realign your spirituality. Your spiritual universe consists of seven zones or, seven types of oracle energies. This journey is about your spiritual universe and understanding how the oracle energies play a role in the health and well-being of your spirituality.

All Aboard

Everything you need to continue this journey has been safely secured in a compartment in your tool kit. If, at any time, you feel overwhelmed, you can return to Chapters 1 and 2 for a refresher course. Help and guidance are a click or a page away. Always remember that you are not—and will never—be alone during this journey. At the end of this journey, you will be in a position to help others who have been on the same spiritual struggle bus. Be a beacon of light in the spiritual universe by helping curious and overwhelmed people. Share the knowledge of what you have learned to help others. This is a gift that needs to be shared, and you have that ability.

It is now time to take the plunge and leap into the next part of your journey. This is your journey, and you are the conductor, coordinator, and tour guide to your spiritual universe. You are going to learn how to understand your body. You are going to learn how to appreciate the significance of the spirituality of your mind, body, and soul. No one can enter your sacred and special place, but you can share your gifts with those that your soul recognizes as being in need. Accept and embrace this journey, and always believe in yourself.

Chapter 3:

Earth: The Center of Your Spiritual Universe

Did you know that the earth is the center of the universe? Without earth, humans, animals, plants, or marine life wouldn't be in existence. The same applies to your body. Your body is your universe. Can you imagine what would happen if you didn't have bones, muscles, organs, or veins? You would be left with an empty vessel, and you would cease to exist. Every part of your body, from the crown of your head down to your toes—and everything in between—is holding you together. You may be wondering if the unwanted pounds, the extra toe, or the skin tags are necessary for your physical universe. I do believe that the answer would be *yes*. Every person is put together the way they are because it was part of God's divine plan for you.

God's plan for you, the day that you were born, was to bless you with a clean spiritual slate. I like to think that this is your personalized stamp of approval for being so unique. There will be no judgment, finger-pointing, or shame for the years between when you were born to where you are now. Everything that happens or happened is part of an ultimate plan. Always remember that there is no such thing as the perfect person walking around on this earth. I believe that the perfect person lives in a fairy tale.

We know and understand that the universe can't exist without the earth. You know that your body can't survive without bones, organs, and all the mechanics that allow for functionality. The time has arrived to inspect the foundation of your spiritual universe. Together, we are going to explore the seven spiritual energies that occupy various zones in your spiritual universe. Please remember that you can return to Chapters 1 and 2 at any time for a little spiritual refresher. Utilize the self-help guides of your tools to ensure that you don't become overwhelmed during the journey. You are the conductor and tour guide, and you have the power to pull the emergency brakes if and when needed to refocus.

Symbolism of the Earth

Spirituality is something everyone either embraces or fights against. Many times it is an internal struggle that leaves one feeling empty, alone, and unsure of what should be happening. I have heard people talking about how exhausted their souls are after going through something trying or traumatic. Some people have shared that they don't have the physical energy or mental capability to continue with their spiritual journeys. I have often wondered how they would come to their conclusions. Who made them experts in self-diagnosing that their spiritual universe was being compromised? You can't walk into the doctor's office and say that something is wrong with your spirit. Whatever is going on with your spirit is between you and your deity.

Representative of the Earth

People won't hesitate to tell you that their interpretation of earth is the ground they walk on or the sand they feel between their toes when walking barefoot. They may even go as far as to say that the earth includes nature. There would be no ground, sand, or nature if the earth was not present. I do believe we are on the same page with our interpretations. Earth is the foundation on which everything we do is based.

I think that humans are afraid to explore what they can't see. They are even more afraid of what they feel, because it is pretty hard to control what can't be seen. They may even feel as if their hands have been chopped off and their sight has been removed because they are powerless. We navigate life by believing what has been taught to us from the time we could understand right from wrong. Most people don't even bother questioning their journey through life because of the trust they have in the people who raised them. Others, well, they have started questioning everything because they aren't afraid to be curious. I may even be so bold as to say that their curiosity rocked the epicenter of their loved ones' earth.

What does the earth mean to you? What do you believe it represents in your spiritual universe? Different religions have different variations of what they believe. My research pulled me in many different directions, and I was left frustrated and defeated. None of the information I researched added up to what the Hindus or Buddhists were saying compared to spiritualists. The best idea I could come up with was to give you various types of examples so that you could build a spiritual empire that fits your requirements.

The Earth as a Female

I had a chuckle when I wrote this heading, because it made me think of those who would say that the world doesn't revolve around women or that women are better at everything. I can promise you that it didn't even register that it may be sexist and offend some people. I added it because I always refer to Mother Nature when something nature-related happens. As humans, we don't respect nature the way we should. I find myself wondering if fires, floods, earthquakes, hurricanes, locust plagues, or droughts are the earth's way of letting us know that we need to be more nurturing, respectful, and caring.

I believe that Mother Nature is trying to tell us something. Unfortunately, we are like unruly children who don't listen to our parents. We ignore the warnings and do what we do best; we ignore our peers. Disaster strikes and everyone starts pointing fingers and the blame game starts. Questions of why wasn't this, that, or the other done, are flung around. Others will lay the blame on whatever deities they believe to be responsible. Some will act out in anger and demand why their deities weren't around when disaster struck. Everyone conveniently forgets the warning signs that were issued. Sorry kids, Mother Nature tried to warn you.

Nurturing and Caring

Over seven billion people in this world have a responsibility to help care for and nurture the earth. We get to do that in many different ways which include not littering, protecting animals and marine life, and taking care of the plant life. Part of our responsibility to the earth is to show kindness to our neighbors. It is a sad state of affairs when not everyone is on the same path, and people carry more responsibilities, don't care, or are maliciously hurting the earth.

The same can be said for our spiritual universe. Each individual has the responsibility to nurture, care for, and nourish their foundations. It is not going to cost you a dime to take care of your foundation. Some people may say that they are not spiritual, but yet they are caring towards others or they go out of their way to ensure others are safe. This is the perfect example of people who are listening to their intuitions. They are feeding their earth by answering their spiritual calling. Are you the grumpy man or lady that lives down the road and calls law enforcement whenever the neighbor's children kick the ball into your yard? If you are, I would like to suggest that you do a little maintenance in your spiritual garden to awaken and realign your spirituality.

Tapping Into Different Spiritual Practices

I needed to think out of the box to give you a variety of perspectives when it comes to spirituality. I know that I can't please everyone. I also know that many will be offended that I dare to group religion and spirituality under one umbrella. I chose to follow my intuition because it is time for everyone to stand together instead of fighting each other. No one—not God, not Allah, not Buddha—wants there to be a divide. No matter what religion you are or which deity you bow down to, we are human beings who share a common interest. It doesn't matter if you are a pagan or a Wiccan practitioner—we all share the same love for humankind, and the world we live in.

It is time to explore the avenues less walked. These avenues may have had signs prohibiting them from strolling down them. I also believe that many found themselves sneaking down these avenues without anyone knowing. The time has come to kick down the signs prohibiting entry to these avenues. You are going to be bold and brave as you grab your broom to clear the debris that will be part of your journey to discover the seven zones of your spiritual universe.

You will see different interpretations based on the recommendations of spiritual teachings and practices, and I would like you to keep in mind that not everyone will have the same experiences. The information shared is not going to be definitive to your life or circumstances. Everything is open to your interpretations, and what will suit your individual needs. I will issue you with gentle reminders as we continue along this interesting, yet exciting journey. Let's get going as we explore the various spiritual practices, predictions, and teachings based on the seven zones.

The Earth in Color

Many spiritual practices, including oracle card readers, believe that red is the color of earth. Those that don't believe in spiritual practices will argue that earthy colors are represented by greens or browns. The significance of red in the spiritual universe is meant to represent the earth in literal terms. What are your first impressions when you see red? I have heard people react to seeing the color red as being angry or hot, and others have referred to it as being the color of love. It is impossible to get everyone on the same page, and we cannot win an argument with someone who is not prepared to look further.

Your spiritual zone—earth—is your foundation. The color red may act as a reminder or warning that you need to take care of your spiritual core. Seeing the color red around you may be a sign from your spiritual guides as they are trying to get your attention. It could be that your spiritual alignment is slightly off and requires a tune-up.

The Earth in Hinduism and Buddhism

The Hindu and the Buddhist practices of spirituality divide the body into zones. Every part of the body is part of a zone that represents one of the seven spiritual energies. They acknowledge that the earth is the most important energy in the body. They believe that the base of the spine is where the earth zone is situated. It is also the first spiritual zone that lays the foundation for the growth of the mind, body, and soul. The foundation of your spiritual universe is referred to as the root, and the color being represented is red.

Chapter 4:

Water: The Elixir of Life to Your Spiritual Universe

You know that the earth is the center of the universe. You learned that during your school-going years and I mentioned it a couple of times—okay, many times—in the previous chapter. I emphasized the importance of the earth for all humans, animals, plants, and marine life. I also referred to the significance that the earth represents in your spiritual universe, including your physical health and well-being.

The next fork in the railway line is going to see us exploring the water bodies, clearing away all litter and debris, hunting for the hidden water systems, and purifying the water. In an article written by Howard A. Perlman from the United States Geological Survey's (USGS) Water Science School, water occupies approximately 71 percent of the earth. It is believed that most of the water resides in the oceans, which equates to approximately 97 percent (Perlman, 2019). As you can see, you cannot do much with dry land. You have been told multiple times that you need to nurture and maintain the earth. The only logical solution would be to add water for the earth to flourish.

The comparison between the world we live in and what happens in our bodies is very similar. The foundation of the earth's energy is important for us to grow, thrive, and share the products of the fruit we will harvest. You know that water is vitally important for the world we live in, but it is also important for our spiritual health. I would like to take two steps back and take a look at an article that was written for the United States Geological Survey by the Water Science School department. The article shares that the human body is made up of approximately 60 percent water. Further, it is believed that water weight makes up approximately 90 percent of the body (Water Science School, 2019). How important is water to our physical health and well-being? I would be so bold as to say that we probably wouldn't be in existence without water.

Water is the elixir of life to the world we live in, as well as the spiritual host in our souls. Water is a gift that needs to be respected. Can you imagine living in a country or a state that allows people to collect three gallons of water a day? That water has to cook meals, provide drinking water, and ensure that the need for hygiene is taken care of. You get people who are frivolous with water and won't hesitate to fill up a swimming pool, or let the water run because they forgot to turn it off. Water is a precious commodity for the world we live in. Remember, we have to use this water to nurture and maintain the earth, as well as rely on it for our spiritual growth.

The Symbolism of Water

There is so much information about water and spirituality that one doesn't know where to start. Water offers tranquility in the way it moves, the blended coloring, and its location. I have spoken to many people who have told me that they would go to the beach for a stroll, find a quiet spot to watch the waves as they crash against the rocks, or relax on the sand to gather their troubled thoughts. The beach may not be an option for many people, though, which is why rivers and lakes are excellent substitutes for water therapy. Not everyone has the luxury of heading off to the nearest body of water for reasons such as living in a desert or that they are in care facilities. Technology, whether you love it or hate it, has made it accessible to bring the peaceful and soothing sounds of water to your digital device.

Did you know that the word 'water' is mentioned 722 times in the Bible? Dwight Tucker Jr. wrote an article for his personal blog, *The Connection*, where he notes that water is the most used word. He goes on to mention that the word 'water' is mentioned more times than the words worship, faith, prayer, and hope (Tucker, 2014). I believe that it is obvious that water has, is, and always will be vitally important in every part of our lives. Water is important to nurture and sustain the environment, for personal use, religious purposes, and to our spirituality.

The Significance of Water in Different Parts of Our Lives

I wanted to include some memories that someone shared with me when speaking about water. They were reminiscing about their childhood days before modern-age technology in the form of television, gaming devices, and digital electronics occupied their time and energy. Many children don't know what it is like to be without a television, a mobile phone, or a gaming device. No shame on anyone when I say that the television was used as a babysitter while Mom quickly ran through the house with the vacuum cleaner. I would almost lay a pile of money on a bet that *Barney*, the purple dinosaur, was the most utilized virtual babysitter across the world. Love him or hate him, he taught our kids how to be kind, how to sing, and how to love each other with a great big, squishy hug.

The memories that were shared had me blink back tears, because these are childhood memories that I enjoyed with friends, family, and neighborhood children. It shows that we knew how to have a good time without worrying about what others thought. We didn't worry about getting dirty while we were making mud cakes. We ran around in the rain and didn't worry about getting our hair wet just before going to church. We would kick off our shoes after the rainstorm had passed to go and jump in the puddles. We didn't have a worry in the world about messing up our perfectly manicured nails or pedicured toes. One of the best memories that involved water was diving into a bathtub full of bubbles and emerging warm and squeaky clean.

You may be thinking that the memories I shared have nothing to do with the significance of water. And you are right, because water—whether falling from the sky, coming through our taps, or being purchased in containers—may not seem significant. As the world expands and the population increases, the memories that many carry close to their hearts will become illusions because we have forgotten that water is part of our lives. We have forgotten how to show respect for something we have been given as a gift. You have a responsibility to take care of a gift that you are given. We live in a society where we take things for granted and pass them off as *it is our right*, instead of *it is a privilege*, to have something.

I want to show you the different ways in which water is used in spirituality. I want to show you how water is used to strengthen your spiritual universe. You are going to learn about the benefits water has on your mind, body, and soul. I am going to share the symbolism of water as practiced by alternative faiths. I want to equip you with the knowledge that you will need to educate others about water. It is time for everyone to learn and show respect for this precious elixir of life that we call water.

Religious Practices

We live in a world that accommodates many different types of religions. Each religion has its own set of requirements that its congregations abide by or believe in. The same applies to spiritual practitioners who rely on their deities for guidance. I have discovered that water is used by everyone, regardless of which side of the spiritual fence they are sitting on. Water is used as a spiritual cleanse, for its healing properties, or as a blessing.

The Hindu population of India believes that the Ganges River is the spiritual body of their beloved goddess Ganga. Local residents and tourists to India visit the Ganges River to experience the healing and cleansing of their souls. The Hindus regularly participate in rituals on the banks of the river, or participate in full-body immersions. It is their belief that practicing these rituals will cleanse their souls of impurities and bad luck. They believe that they will be blessed with good fortune, health, and luck (Das, 2019).

All members in the Muslim faith are required to follow a mandatory cleansing procedure. This cleansing is known as wudu or purification with water. It is a mandatory practice that is performed prior to their daily prayers (Bhimji, 2016). The following scripture from passage 5:6 of the Qur'an, as written by the prophet Muhammed, describes this procedure: "O you who have faith! When you stand up for prayer, wash your faces and your hands up to the elbows, and wipe a part of your heads and your feet, up to the ankles. If you are junub, purify yourselves. But if you are sick, or on a journey, or any of you has come from the toilet, or you have touched women, and you cannot find water, then make *tayammum* with clean ground and wipe a part of your faces and your hands with it. Allah does not desire to put you to hardship, but He desires to purify you, and to complete His blessing upon you so that you may give thanks," (The Quran, n.d.).

Water is used for many religious practices. Faith-based religious denominations use water for blessings such as babies or people who are dying, or full-body water immersion baptisms. The Roman Catholic Church uses holy water, which is symbolic to them. They believe that the holy water is a sign of purification and protection, which is why members make a cross as they enter the church. Holy water is also used in rituals such as baptisms and the blessing of members. Some older orthodox religions believe that ancient springs have healing powers, or are miracle cures for diseases or illnesses. Members of these older religions consume the blessed water before they practice their morning prayers. Some even go as far as to add holy water when they are preparing their meals.

Spiritual Meanings

The water you utilize doesn't care what faith you are, or what religion you practice. It doesn't care about any of the hundreds, if not thousands, of alternative religious or spiritual practices. Water is the elixir of life that needs to be respected. I have previously touched on going to the beach and watching the water roll onto the beach, or sitting on the riverbank staring out at the water as it moves around. These two actions are more spiritual than you would care to believe. They are healing to the mind and soul which, in turn, is positive for the body.

What would you say if I told you that water holds spiritual messages? Human beings are conditioned to see what they want to see, and hear what they want to hear. I have heard people mention that they only see what is in front of them, and that is all the affirmations that they need. Some have said that they were lazy and didn't take notice of the finer details. And then, I have had people tell me that they are more observant than what they should be and see things that others don't. They also say that they are always looking for the meanings or reasons behind what they are seeing. Let's take a look at some of the spiritual meanings and messages that water brings to our lives.

You know that you consume water because you're thirsty, but have you ever stopped to consider why you choose water over soda, coffee, or milkshakes? The spiritual takeaway would be that you care about what happens in your life. It was a sign, when you chose to drink the water over everything else, that you are optimistically cautious when deciding the fate of future or career choices.

Not many people will pay attention to the water overflowing from the cup, bucket, or bath. Have you ever stopped to think about how it makes you feel when you see wastage? The spiritual takeaway would indicate that you cannot control every situation. It is believed that seeing water being spilled in visions, dreams, or in person refers to your emotions or coping with potentially volatile situations such as anger management issues. The vision of overflowing water is a reminder that you need to accept that things happen for a reason. Find the peace within you to ground your emotions before they bubble over.

Water comes in many types of vessels which range from bottles, cups, and buckets to lakes, rivers, and oceans. I know that I am stating the obvious, but it is important to get a visual representation of water in words that will help you understand the concepts of water being flexible. The spiritual takeaway would indicate that you need to allow for flexibility in your life. Stop following the same boxed ritual day in and day out, and allow yourself the space to step out of your comfort zone. Dare to be free and flexible without worrying about fitting in all the time. I have heard people say that, "a change is as good, if not better, than a vacation."

These are only a couple of the messages I have shared with you, but it follows a pattern that speaks into your life or situation. I have mentioned it multiple times, and now may be an ideal time for a gentle reminder that you don't have to restrict your feelings or follow the beliefs of anyone else. This journey that you are on is personal to you. You don't have to share your journey with anyone. One day, when the time is right, you will be ready to share; and on that day, your light will shine as all seven of the oracle and spiritual energies will shine through you.

Tapping Into Different Spiritual Practices

We are ready to stomp the grounds of the streams less waded through. We are ignoring the warning signs that prohibit us from entering the area, because it is our right to explore. Together we are going to kick down those signs as we continue on this spiritual journey. This part of the journey is going to have you grabbing a net, because you are going to remove the litter that is preventing the water from flowing. You are going to be a professional at navigating your way through spiritual blockages and cleansing treatments by the time you reach the end of Chapter 9.

The gentle reminder is in effect as I reiterate that the spiritual teachings and practices that follow are open to interpretation. Not everything that is mentioned is based on your situation or circumstances. Let's get going as we continue on this journey where we will take an alternative look at what water represents to our spiritual universe.

Water in Color

What color do you associate with water? Many would answer without even thinking, and say that it is blue. Others would say that it is colorless. Technically, you would be correct on both accounts. When you look at photos of the ocean, the water is all shades of blue. When you pour water from the tap, it is colorless.

Spiritual practices believe that the energy of water is represented by the color orange. I believe that earth and water, and red and orange, have a very close connection. This connection spills over into the spiritual universe where our feelings and emotions are closely connected. There is a barrier between the earth (dry) and water (wet) energy that points to a boundary and a mutual agreement that the two should not commingle. Unfortunately, nature becomes a little detached from the original brief, and boundaries will be crossed which may cause damage.

We resemble the earth and water in our personal and spiritual lives. We all have boundaries that protect us. Nothing stops you from testing the limits of the boundaries, but you have to be prepared for the fallout if things don't go according to plan. You want to create healthy connections with friends, family, and/or partners which may include intimacy, feelings, and the all-important boundaries. Return to your tool kit of tips and guides when you begin to feel that boundaries are being crossed, or that you are feeling uneasy about a situation.

Water in Hinduism and Buddhism

The Hindu and the Buddhist spiritual practices have the water zone located below the navel. It is believed to be precisely three inches below the belly button. Many spiritual practitioners have put a lot of emphasis on connections which, when comparing it to the Hindu and Buddhist practices, relates to sexual and intimacy desires. It is important to keep your spiritual universe free of blockages by taking care of your spiritual alignment. Always remember to be kind to yourself, which is why self-care is so important.

Chapter 5:

Fire: The Eternal Flame of Your Spiritual Universe

Your spiritual basket of energies is beginning to take shape. The knowledge that you are gathering along this journey is preparing you for the final destination—putting all the energies to work in one vessel. We are going to continue this journey by exploring the third energy in your spiritual universe. The next fork in the railway line is going to see you dodging flames, and avoiding being scorched by fire.

You may be wondering how I went from the earth and water to fire. You don't see the association. Stick around for this, because I will explain it further in this chapter. You may be thinking that fire has no place in your spiritual universe. What comes to mind when you think or hear about fire? Thanks to the scaremongering tactics of parents, friends, family, or educators, you may associate fire with the pits of hell where evil and demonic spirits reside. You may be thinking that fire is associated with death and destruction. What good is fire for our spiritual health and well-being when it causes death and destruction in the world we live in?

You may not know it, but fire is one of the elements of nature. I do understand the confusion when it comes to the topic of fires. Wildfires are necessary to help prepare the ecosystem for growth, change, and new life. These types of fires are planned, controlled, and actioned according to the area's climate conditions. As you may know, nature is pretty unpredictable, and accidents happen. In this instance, even though contained, a gust of wind may pick up an ember and carry it to a dry area. What follows then is a natural disaster, because—even when controlled—it can become a dangerous and costly operation.

On the other side of the fire fence, you have the accidental fire starters and arsonists. I hesitate to use the term accidental, because most people will tell you that it was an accident when they threw their cigarette butt out of the window while driving. Others will say that they were having such a wonderful time that they forgot to pick up their glass bottles after their outdoor party in the forest. Arsonists are deliberate fire starters who participate in criminal practices. Arsonists start fires with malicious intent to cause harm to a person, to destroy someone's home or property, or to destroy an area of land (U.S. Forest Service, 2019).

I am not going to tell you to ignore what is happening in nature. However, this book is not about the world at large, it is about you and your spiritual journey through life. You have questions and you want to know more about what is going on in your spiritual universe. I am here, as your partner in curiosity, to help you understand everything that you are learning, in simple and easy-to-understand terms. Are you ready to proceed with this journey? Let's explore the next leg of our journey to see what fire represents to our spiritual lives.

The Symbolism of Fire

Have you ever thought about what the role fire plays in your everyday life? Yes, you use the toaster to toast the bread. Yes, you boil water in the kettle to make your tea or coffee. Yes, you use your stove to prepare your meals. Yes, you use your barbecue grill to cook your meat. Technically, we use electrical appliances that do the same job that a fire would—but what does this mean for our spiritual universe? Does fire represent the idea that we fill our bodies with food and beverages? Have I just planted a seed of wonder in your spiritual universe and watered it with the elixir of life? My curiosity has been tickled, because I have never thought about the association between fire and my spiritual life.

We have learned that fire is one of the four main elements of nature. We know that fire occupies one of the seven spiritual zones in our bodies. And yes, we are well aware that fire also includes one of the seven energies in our spiritual universe. I spoke about fire in the literal sense, and what it means to the environment and the ecosystem. Fire, if not controlled, could cause death and destruction. What does fire mean for your spiritual universe? That is a question that I am hoping to understand and explore alongside you.

The Power of Fire in Your Spiritual Universe

The seed of wonder is beginning to grow roots. You are trying to find the fire in your soul. The curiosity buttons in your spiritual universe are being pushed to find this fire. The other part of your mind is looking for any indications as to what this fire is doing or meant to do. Fire is used in most faith-based religions, as well as in spiritual practices and personal use. What we know about fire is that it is, and has been, a part of our lives since the beginning of time. Fire is mentioned in the Bible, it is used in the titles of movies or lyrics of music, or as symbols or logos.

I believe that it is safe to assume that not everyone will have the same interpretation of fire. With that being said, everything I am writing about is open to interpretation. I believe that I have dropped many reminders that you are in control of your choices and the decisions you make. You may have an *aha* moment where something is said or referred to that resonates with an experience or a memory that you have had. I have mentioned that I have never given any thought to the idea of fire in my spiritual universe. Not even the research and speaking to people have prepared me for the idea of fire deep in my soul. Many people have been through the religious and spiritual mills. Most know about that burning feeling in their souls—no, it is not heartburn. The sensation cannot be explained, but it becomes warmer as your passion or belief in something grows stronger. I am only learning now, as I scrub through so many different resources, that the fire burning in my soul represents my passion for wanting to help people.

Fire in the world around us is meant to be an element that balances nature. Unfortunately, we don't see fire for the purpose of which it was created. Instead, we are witnesses to the death and devastating destruction that can ensue—whether natural, accidental, or criminal. One could almost say that it is impossible to see the good in fire because we see and hear what the media portray during news coverage. I can understand the hesitancy of comparing literal fire with spiritual fire. Yes, the two are worlds apart, but we are creatures of habit who become overwhelmed when hearing trigger words.

There is no shame in what you believe, have, or haven't believed. Maybe you have never had the courage to ask questions relating to that burning sensation deep in your soul. Maybe you tried reaching out to someone you trusted who dismissed your query about the fire burning within you. I'm sorry that you were made to feel afraid, insignificant, or unworthy of answers. This is one of the many reasons why I wanted to write the books I have. I wanted to give (or at least attempt to give) you answers that are always open to interpretation. This book has no firepits or rings of fire that you will be thrown into. Remember, you entered a zone that is free of bullying, judgment, and condemnation. Now let's move this party along and have a look at what fire may represent to your spiritual universe.

The Stories as Explained by Fire

We have established that the world does not consist of one or two types of people. The world is home to billions of people from different ethnic groups, cultures, spiritual practices, and religions. Everyone will have an opinion about what something means to them, their lives, their cultures, or their beliefs. The main focus of this chapter is to look at the spiritual meaning of fire in your life. The first order of business is to look at what fire may symbolize in your life, and also in the world around you:

- heat
- flames
- death
- destruction
- anger
- passion
- desire
- new beginnings
- hope
- growth
- purifying

You can amend this list to include anything you feel fire represents to your life. Each word that you can think of that represents fire is a message from your spiritual universe. Each of the words can be interpreted in whichever way you see fit. Every feeling you express comes from your soul. I want you to make up a mantra or words of affirmation before you continue with the next paragraph. Here is an example of what you could use: "I am going to stop doubting myself. I am the strongest, and most courageous person in my world. I am not a weak person. My spiritual universe embraces me as I am, warts, freckles, and all." Believe what you have written in your mantra. Write it down on sticky notes, and put them all around your home where you can be reminded every day. Come on, let's take a close look at the messages your spiritual universe has been trying to tell you.

Seeing and hearing the flames as they crackle and pop would likely be an indication that your soul is hurting. Someone may have said something to upset you, or you may have seen something that angered you. Some people are verbal when the angry switch is activated, but others keep their anger to themselves. This anger will grow until you can't hold it back. You will pour out all the anger you have been repressing. The anger coming from within you has the power to burn bridges that weren't meant to be burned. Your tongue and voice are incredibly powerful, and can be destructive tools. Don't fill your spiritual universe with anger and hatred. Douse the fire before it gets to the point of no return.

I would like you to think about a pressure cooker. The concept behind the cooker is to prepare your meat or vegetables in the minimum amount of time. You fill the cooker with water, add whatever you want to cook, sprinkle with spices, pop on the lid, set the timer and temperature, and you leave the cooker to work its magic. Direct your attention to the person who makes you go weak at the knees. It may be your spouse, your partner, or someone you hope to fill the void in your life. What happened when you met the object of your desire? Most people talk about feeling flutters deep in the trenches of their stomachs, and others refer to feeling a fire warming them from the inside. The fire will become more intense as your feelings grow, or it will continue burning with desire for your partner. For those who have been in a relationship for a long time and don't feel that fire, awaken and realign your spiritual universe with the tools you have been given in Chapters 2 and 3.

One of my favorite messages from my spiritual universe involves a combination of hope, new beginnings, and growth. This is something everyone has experienced in their lives without realizing it. I reached out for help from someone I met while writing my second book about angels. This person had experienced the loss of a beloved family member. They explained that it felt as if the torch within their spiritual universe had been snuffed out. Their world had exploded, and I remember them telling me that their soul was exhausted. They were convinced that their soul had died. Everyone around them was being diagnosed with illnesses—some were admitted to the hospital for health conditions, and others passed away for no apparent reason. They apologized multiple times for being so dramatic, and I could hear the pain and anguish—as well as exhaustion—in their voice. Three months after the death of their family member, and living in darkness, their spiritual fire came back to life. The family member came to this person in a dream, and told them that they need to get out of the darkness. They told them to walk toward the flame flickering in their soul. They then told them to wipe away the tears and look around. What they saw was a display of new perspectives which symbolized hope and new beginnings. The fire had never gone out... it was just put on pause until they were ready to find their way back. This person had grown during a time when they had almost given up. They found their way back and, today, that person is sharing their experience and positivity with those who need it.

Tapping Into Different Spiritual Practices

Stop! Wait! Don't reach for the fire extinguisher or the bottle of antacid just yet. I would like you to don your fire-resistant cloak and boots, and join me on the next leg of your journey through your spiritual universe. Many people feel intimidated when exploring alternative practices, and many may not care what others think because they know that it is their life. Many *do* care because they don't want to be an embarrassment to others in their circle. One person I spoke to said that they don't share their beliefs with others because then there will be no arguments. I do rather like the idea of keeping religious or spiritual statuses private; because as with politics, everyone has the right to their personal choices.

You are most probably experiencing flutters deep within your soul. You know that those flutters are symbolic of the flickering of a flame. You are aware that no one can ever snuff out that flame, because you are in control. You are a unique individual who should not be people-pleasing to keep others happy at your expense. Your spiritual flame will continue flickering, regardless of the path you are on, until you are ready to give it the attention it is seeking. Let's take a look at what other spiritual practices have to say about the eternal flame that resides in your soul. Remember that everything that is mentioned in the following paragraphs is open to interpretation.

Fire in Color

You know that fire is one of the elements of nature. You know that fire, in the literal sense, is all shades ranging from an angry red to an intense orange color. We have all seen the flames dancing around in the firepit, a fireplace, or in raging wildfires. I believe it would make sense if the energy of fire in the spiritual universe would follow the world around us. The spiritual universe offers a different perspective when it comes to matters of the soul.

Spiritual practitioners believe that the energy of fire is represented by the color yellow. The color palette of your spiritual universe is taking shape. Each stop along your spiritual journey is giving you a sneak peek before you put all the pieces of the puzzle together. It is believed that the fire energy of the color yellow in your spiritual universe is the sun (or light) that shines to make the darkness disappear. Your spiritual universe is slowly but surely beginning to take shape. The sun, or the color yellow, is lighting the darkness of the earth in order to see the ebb and flow of the tides in the center of your spiritual universe.

Fire Energy in Hinduism and Buddhism

The Hindu and the Buddhist practices of spirituality are divided into various zones within your body. Each of the zones accommodates one of the seven energies. The third energy, which has been identified as fire energy, is encased in an area behind your navel and below your rib cage. This area is also referred to as the solar plexus, which many believe is where those pesky gut feelings or intuitions are conjured from. Oh, we love to hate those gut feelings—but if we have to be honest with ourselves, they do their best to keep us on the straight and narrow.

Spiritualists believe that the yellow energy within our spiritual universe is a sign of strength, intelligence, assertiveness, and willpower. I love this assessment, because this is what I have been saying since I started writing this book. Every single person walking around on this earth is special and possesses unique qualities. I cannot wait to get to the end of this journey, when we will put all the pieces we have collected together. That final picture is going to give you all the confidence and power you need to shine your multi-colored light of all things beautiful. All you need to do, and I will continue reminding you, is to practice self-care by keeping your spirit aligned.

Chapter 6:

Love: The Universal Language of Your Spiritual Universe

Everyone has been in love, but not everyone has experienced *true* love. Many don't understand the concept of love, and many more will argue until they are hoarse that love does not exist. Even more will say that they are experts on the subject of love while they have never been married, nor have they been in a relationship with anyone. Everyone is entitled to their decisions, choices, or beliefs of what love means to them. I am not here to choose sides, and I am certainly not here to force you to believe in something you can't or don't want to.

I realize and understand that most people may be offended by other people's opinions. I also know that what may follow are heated arguments that could cause more damage than what it is worth. We may not all be on the same page when it comes to the sensitive topic of love, so this is where I turn to my trusted online dictionary for some assistance. You have to get a feeling and an understanding of what love is before you can welcome and embrace it in your spiritual universe. The definition of love is based on various types of feelings or emotions that are buried within the depths of our souls.

The Merriam-Webster dictionary shows us that love has many definitions. The definitions are like pieces of putty that can be tweaked to fit in with the circumstances you are in. The first definition of love is built on the foundation of affection. Love is a feeling that is experienced when you look at your children or partner, and know that you would walk over a field of thorns, hot coals, and glass shards to protect them. Love is also that unexplainable jolt in the pit of your stomach when you realize that you have indescribable feelings of affection for your partner, or children.

Hearing the words: "I love you," is something that a lot of people don't understand. How can you tell someone that you love them when you don't understand what love is? You don't need to be involved in a relationship or be family to tell someone that you love them. As you have learned, love is a feeling based on affection. Next time you are on the phone with your friend and it is time to end that call, let them know that you love them. They will understand what you are saying; you're telling them that you are thankful that they are in your life (Merriam-Webster, 2019b).

The word love is attached to something or someone you are enthusiastic about, such as your love for coffee, reading, writing, or going for hikes. You don't have to be afraid to use the word love. You are the author of your life journey, and you have the authority to change the course of your journey. You get to choose your feelings, because you are in control. I'm not going to try and sway your mind. I am not going to try and force you to love Oreo's when your favorite is Chips Ahoy. I am not here to give you relationship advice, because I am not a therapist. I am here to share my spiritual insights and interpretations with you based on real life experiences. Love just happens to be one of the seven energies that has a place in our spiritual universe.

It is time to put the definitions, assumptions, and interpretations aside for now. We are going to take a look at what love symbolizes in faith-based religions and spiritual beliefs. I would like to remind you that love is not about a cute little cherub angel that flutters around and stamps you with a heart-shaped arrow. You will not see little heart fireworks. No hearts will bounce up at you as you continue reading this chapter. What you may feel—if you have not already picked up on it—is the huge amount of caring and compassion that this book is created with. Your thoughts and feelings have been swaddled in copious amounts of love that don't need, nor care, for reciprocation. My publisher, my editor, and myself are selfless people who believe that we have enough love to embrace millions of people. We love you, and thank you for being on this journey with us.

The Symbolism of Love

What do you think about when you see the word love? What does it symbolize to you? What does it say about you? These are questions that you can answer for yourself. You may not have the answers at this moment. You may only have an answer when you reach the end of the chapter. This is not a quiz and no one is going to grade your answers. We have established that not everyone will have the same experiences. Feelings and emotions are based on you as an individual. Love is a four-letter word that carries the weight of the world on its shoulders.

I have spoken to many people during the research phase of my books. Some have said that if they wanted to understand the true meaning of the word love, they had to learn to love themselves first. Their reasoning behind their answer was spot on. Without a moment's hesitation, they said that they couldn't share their love with someone or something else if they didn't know how to apply it to themselves. I am reminded of a parrot who will repeat what you have said after weeks, months, or years of saying the same thing. We become programmed and conditioned to say something without understanding the meaning behind it. We say it so often that it loses its flair and becomes an automated, robotic response that is free of emotions.

I'm not going to tell you that love doesn't exist. As you are reading this, your intuition sensor is starting to draw some power deep down inside your soul. I like to believe that the love that is inside each person was placed there from the time you were born. I am aware that not everyone experienced a happy childhood. The love you received may have come from your birth parents, or it may have come from the person who raised you or cared for you. I once had a young gentleman tell me that his birth mom loved him so much that she gave him to another mom who would love him even more. He said that he had so much love in his belly that he could share it with the whole world. Love is embedded in each of us. No one is going to shine the spotlight on you because you don't feel it. All we need to do is clear the litter and trim back the branches that have formed a barricade around the love zone in your spiritual universe.

Understanding the Power of Love in Your Spiritual Universe

Did you know that this is the fourth stop on the journey to the discovery of your spiritual universe? We are halfway through this journey—and this subject is, by far, the hardest. Everyone may claim to be an expert on the subject of love, and many may tell you their theories about where love originated. I like to believe that love originated with our Creator—God; but you can believe in whichever deity you choose to. I would like to acknowledge that my opinion might not meet with everyone's approval, and many may argue. I believe that I have proven that I am not choosing sides when it comes to religion and spiritual beliefs and practices. This book is an excellent example of non-biased opinions.

In Chapter 4, I mentioned that water is mentioned 722 times in the Bible, which is believed to be more than love. The exact number of times love is mentioned remains unclear, because of the number of versions that the Bible is written in. That was when I decided to take a step back and go to the origin of where life is believed to have begun. I know of many people who say that they are not loved, that they are not worthy of being loved, or that they have never experienced love. I would like to show you a passage from the Bible which (whether you believe it to be true or not) I believe is a true testimony of love for you, me, and everyone from different religious or spiritual backgrounds, ethnicity, or gender.

The Bible is jam-packed full of scriptures and stories that have been written for us. I know that when I open the Bible, I am almost always directed to a verse that seems to answer a question I have. I had someone tell me that mediums or card readers believe that the cards they draw are equivalent to the messages in the Bible. I had a question, and when I looked at the bible verses 1 John 3:16–18, taken from the New International Version (NIV), they jumped up at me; "This is how we know that love is: Jesus Christ laid down his life for us. And we ought to lay down our lives for our brothers and sisters. If anyone has material possessions and sees a brother or sister in need but has no pity on them, how can the love of God be in that person? Dear Children, let us not love with words or speech but with actions and in truth."

First Love Yourself

It is time to start clearing the barricade of weeds and litter that is holding your spiritual universe hostage. In the physical world, you would use shears, chemicals, or gardeners to clear your garden—but none of those will work in your spiritual universe. The most efficient tools, chemicals, and help you can find are yourself. You have to love yourself before the barricades will fall away. I know that it is a tall order. You are most probably one of the millions who believe that you are not worthy of your love. You may be one of the millions who use their past mistakes and judgments as an excuse to hide behind the barricades.

I want you to read this and understand what I am telling you. Your past is gone, and it cannot be brought back. What you are feeling is the carbon copy of what happened. It is time to let that carbon copy go, because you cannot do anything about it. You have to accept that you can't change what happened. The beauty of the lives we live is that you learn many lessons. Those lessons are what your present and future are based on. Accept that the past is where it belongs—in the past. Don't waste time on yesterday; but take what you learned yesterday, and add it to today so that tomorrow will be even better.

I would like to give you a couple of tips to help you show yourself some love. This list is an example that you can build on and find more ways to show yourself that you are worthy of loving and being loved:

- Stop being a people pleaser; use that dainty little two-letter word that makes people's jaws drop to the ground at your boldness to use it.
- There is only one *you* in this world; claim your right to stand on your pedestal so that everyone can focus their attention on you.
- It is perfectly fine to make mistakes; nobody is perfect and you won't be struck down by a bolt of lightning.
- Forgive yourself when you don't reach your expectations of yourself; always remember that tomorrow is another day.
- Live, laugh, and have fun; please know that the world will not stop turning if you take time for yourself.
- Kick pride out of your life; there is no room for pride when love is stepping up to the plate.

The tips I have shared with you are a drop in the ocean of how you can find love in yourself. I can go on and tell you that you could cover your home in sticky notes filled with positive affirmations. I could tell you that you shouldn't hide away from bullies, but rather stand up and put them in their place. I could even direct you to the mirror so that you can stare at yourself and repeat a mantra that you are who you are, that you will always be who you are, and that you are worthy of self-love. Yes, I could tell you all these things to help you see the flame of love peeping through the blockade in your soul but—oh wait, I did just tell you!

Symbols of Love

What do you associate love with? Everyone would agree that love represents the doodle of the heart. What would you say if I told you that the actual organ, known as the heart, doesn't resemble the image we see displayed on Valentine's Day or in the emojis on instant messengers? I'm not going to tell you that you are wrong about your association, because I want you to believe whatever resonates with you. I would, however, like to show you that love symbolizes more than hearts. Let's take a look to see what other symbols could be associated with love:

- being gifted with a bunch of flowers, or buying them for yourself
- being gifted with photos or ornaments depicting swans, or white doves
- being gifted a Celtic love knot ring or pendant, or gifting it to yourself

- being gifted with a pendant of a shamrock, or purchasing one for yourself

I am reminded of an early 90s rendition of Wet Wet Wet's song, *Love Is All Around*, which was featured in the 1994 movie, *Four Weddings and A Funeral*, starring Andie McDowell and Hugh Grant in the lead. The first stanza of the song says: "*I feel it in my fingers, I feel it in my toes, Love that's all around me, And so the feeling grows.*" I believe that the original authors of this song were trying to let people know that love is a feeling that needs to grow before it can be experienced.

Tapping Into Different Spiritual Practices

Your spiritual universe has undergone a transformation. This chapter has been about you and the love you have hidden away. You started clearing away the barricades that were hiding your spiritual love energy from everyone. You have learned that you may love yourself without any judgment. You have also learned that you need to, and deserve to, respect yourself. No more self-bashing yourself, and absolutely no more doubting who you are in your spiritual universe.

I recently had someone tell me that they could never look at themselves in the mirror. They knew that they were overweight, and were constantly being ridiculed by so-called friends and loved ones for it. Their negativity toward them built up years' worth of self-loathing, to the point where they saw disgust in themselves. Something within them clicked after being on the receiving end of the abuse and bullying. Without any word to anyone, they approached the mirror with trepidation. It took a couple of weeks before they were comfortable with looking at themselves. The first day that they could look at themselves for longer than five minutes was the day that they broke down and cried. The tears that flowed were like a tidal wave of emotions being spilled. They said that it was an instantaneous feeling of healing that started to take place within them. Now this person is at the point where they stand before the mirror each morning and evening, and enjoy a full-on conversation with themself. This person learned to love themself so much that the extra pounds they were carrying around started melting away. The moral of this story is to assure you that it is—and will never—be too late to love yourself.

Love in Color

I can only imagine what goes through your mind when you get to this section of each chapter, and guess your answer before reading further. I can also imagine your frustration that none of the colors have corresponded with the different elements. If your x-ray vision was working right now, you would see me with my hands in the air and a frown on my brow. Let's confuse our already confused minds by comparing what we were taught, to what the spiritualists believe. What is the color that you associate with love? I believe that almost everyone's answers would be unanimous when they say red, shades of red, and pink.

I have learned, that while writing this book, nothing surprises me anymore. We used the color red at the beginning of this spiritual journey when we discovered that the earth energy was red. That can only mean that red is crossed off the list. I will stop guessing which color follows, because I'm enjoying these new revelations. I do believe that it proves how conditioned we really are. Human beings are like sponges who just take in everything that is told to us. I think we have reached a point where we have no energy to argue, because of the fear of being discriminated against. And that is sad, but I am holding onto hope that this life journey of discovering your spiritual universe will give us all the courage to do what we were put on this earth to do.

The color associated with the oracle and spiritual energy of love is green. Spiritualists believe that green represents compassion, caring, love, and empathy. We may associate green as being part of nature. One only has to think about the grass, the leaves on the trees after a harsh winter, or seeds peeping and pushing their way through the soil. Yes, I do see why love would be associated with the color green. I am beginning to understand that green is a sign of regrowth and rebirth which can only be associated with love.

Love Energy in Hinduism and Buddhism

The Hindu and Buddhist spiritual practices are most fascinating. They have provided us with a detailed railway map through our spiritual universe. The fourth stop on our journey saw us taking an excursion to understand love in our lives, and your spiritual universe. We have cleared the debris that had caused a blockage in the zone where love would be found. If you were thinking that the love energy zone was located on the left-hand side of your chest; you would be wrong. It is believed that the love energy zone is located in the center of your chest. Hindus and Buddhists believe that this zone provides healing of the mind and soul. It is important to continue practicing self-love and self-care by using your tools, including the new ones added in this chapter. It is up to you to keep your spiritual universe clean and free of blockages.

Chapter 7:

Sound: Creative Communication to Strengthen Your Spiritual Universe

You are just over halfway through your journey of learning how to grow, care for, and utilize your spiritual universe in your life. I do believe that you have had fun clearing your energy zones and rediscovering the gifts you have been hiding. I don't know about you, but I am learning more as I accompany you on this journey. I do believe that this journey will never be boring or become redundant. No matter who you are, or where you are in your life's journey, you will always be learning something new. I find this subject fascinating, and I love how everything is open to interpretation. We tend to go through life following the rules as prescribed, because people are afraid to take a step to the left or right.

The fifth stop on this journey through your spiritual universe may be one of the most challenging you have yet experienced. I do believe that this is a very important part of the journey. Many may find that this leg of the journey will be intimidating, scary, or overwhelming. Others may find that they would require bucket loads of restraint, mountains of filtering, and oceans full of patience. All I want for everyone is that they are comfortable at all times, and have fun learning about what you have hidden deep in your soul. This part of the journey is going to push you outside of your comfort zone, but not in a negative way. Together we are going to discover how to prepare our spiritual universe for greatness.

The first order of business is to ensure that we are ready for the discovery and cleanup part of this journey. Can you remember all the gentle reminders that I have dropped since you started reading this book? The ones where I reassure you that this is a journey free of judgment, bullying, and condemnation? I am going to repeat myself here so that you can understand and know that you shouldn't have to be concerned with what other people think. Let them deal with their insecurities the way they see fit, and *you* deal with *your* life the way you want to live it. No one has the right to tell you what you should be doing. I will assume that you are of age and not in need of consent from anyone if you are reading this book. You are in charge of the discovery and journey of your spiritual universe.

Navigating Your Spiritual Communication Channels

I have a couple of questions I would like to ask you to think about before we go any further. These questions do not require *yes* or *no* answers, but I would like you to think about them.

- Do you hear the sounds around you?
- Do you stop and listen to those sounds?

- Do you look to see where those sounds come from?

I would like you to participate in a little test or experiment when you have a moment or three. You are going to sit yourself down so that you don't get hurt. Next, you are going to close your eyes. Then you are going to listen to the sounds that are around you. What are you hearing?

- Can you hear the tick-tock of the clock on the wall?
- Can you hear the sound of the washing machine reaching the end of its spinning cycle?
- Can you hear the birds chirping in the garden?
- Can you hear the tinkling of the wind chimes that hang in front of your window?

These, and many more, are the sounds that we take for granted. These are everyday sounds we have become immune to. You may be wondering why I am being so dramatic about sounds. You may believe that sounds are just sounds, and that they don't add any value to your life. Have you ever thought about what it would be like if your hearing was taken away from you? Have you ever considered what it would be like to live in a world where you can't even hear your heart beating in your chest? Did you know that millions of people around the world are hearing-impaired, and live their lives in a silent bubble? Why would you take a gift, such as hearing, for granted and not enjoy the birds chirping, the dogs barking, or the cats purring?

I do believe that we have been conditioned to accept whatever is told to us. I have said this in previous chapters, and I will most likely say it again and repeat it in future writings. I recently spoke to someone who is periodically, and without much notice, plunged into the dark ages where they have no power. I never realized how many countries across the world have this problem, which made me realize how much we take for granted. They told me that when their power goes off, they can hear sounds they'd never heard before. The background noise, which I believe is referred to as "white noise," is gone. They described the silence as eerie, but in a good way. I don't know how eerie can be good, but I'm not an expert in that department. They then said that the nighttime power outages are the worst. That is when their senses are heightened, and they believe that they could hear the grass growing.

Listening to Your Spiritual Guides

Have you ever had a conversation with yourself while walking through Target or the crowded mall? You don't realize that you're talking until someone politely says; "Excuse me?" I am confident when I say that most of us have been in these shoes at least once during our lifetime. I remember receiving a meme that read; *"If you see me talking to myself, just move along. I'm self-employed, and having a staff meeting"* (Goodreads, n.d.-b). I know that many people make jokes about 'hearing' voices or changing their minds about certain decisions because something (or someone) told them it was a wrong move. It is instances like this where I believe that our spiritual guides are trying to get our attention.

Maybe it is time to clear the barrier that you have built around your soundproofed room. It is time to open that room, remove the soundproofing decor, and fix the megaphone that you have hidden in the corner. All the channels for communication will be open and free of debris. An open channel means that you can receive any messages that need to be heard without delay. Let's take a little stroll through your soundproofed room to learn how you could clear it out and decorate it to suit your purpose.

Ditch the Devices

Modern technology has made it easy for us to forget about what is going on in other areas of our lives. Devices are a necessary evil in this day and age. Many people use their devices for work, because it is their livelihood and a means to support their families. Others hide behind their devices to block out what is going on in their lives. Let's not forget about all the "Sofa Physicians, Armchair Politicians, and Keyboard Warriors," who graduated with honors from the "University of Google." Love them or hate them, electronic devices were designed for a purpose. They bring friends and family together who aren't able to be in the same city or country. They helped save the day when our lives were turned upside down because of a global pandemic, and allowed people to work from home.

I see the good in everything, but I also see the not-so-good or healthy side of electronic devices. I am not going to tell you to get rid of your devices. I know that the heading for this section says *Ditch the Devices*, but that meant to prepare you for what I wanted to get across to you. Do you know that little voice that whispers in your ear... the one that tells you that you need to take the trash out? You ignore that little voice and continue making TikTok videos. You go to bed, wake up in the morning, and walk into the kitchen to be met with ants crawling on your floor. You want to blame someone, but you remember that the little voice tried to tell you to take the trash out.

I would like to share a couple of tips with you on how you can break your addiction to your electronic devices. An appropriate little disclaimer right here—you will struggle for the first hour, 2 hours, or 25 hours. Don't give up, though—knuckle on through it. I promise you—and I don't make promises very easily—that your device will still be there. The promise goes out the window if you drop your device in the toilet or accidentally put it in the washing machine. It is not easy to break a habit. I hear about people who want to give up smoking—and most do well for about the first 5 hours, but then the wheels start buckling. The best place to be when altering a habit is right there where you are at any given moment in time. You have the choice to limit your screen time. Follow me:

- Choose a cutoff time for when you will put your device away for the evening.
- Find a designated spot for your mobile device.
- Put your device in its designated spot at the cutoff time.
- Start your day by leaving your mobile device in its designated spot.
- Brush your teeth, open the blinds/curtains, and start breakfast.
- Check your phone to see if you have any important messages that need immediate attention.
- Avoid social media on an empty stomach (always ensure that you are nourished before you go to battle).
- Practice meditation, or have your morning shake or coffee out in the garden.
- Acknowledge your spiritual guides and ask for guidance for the day ahead.

- Learn to listen to that little voice that drops multiple hints throughout the day.

I am not saying that you should follow everything I have noted here. These are tips that were compiled after speaking to people who have been where we all are—or have been at—some stage in our lives.

Connecting With Your Spiritual Guides

The importance of caring for your spiritual universe cannot be stressed enough. It is your responsibility to ensure that your spiritual universe is aligned at all times. This is a necessary practice if you want to be present and in line with your spiritual guides. I cannot force you to keep your channels of communication clean and free-flowing. I cannot force you to do anything you don't want to. I can, however, be the support aid that gives you options that you can utilize. Grab your broom, your shovel, or your bottle of multi-purpose cleaner, and let's look over some examples of ways in which you can connect with your spiritual universe:

- Spend time outdoors by gardening, hiking, swimming, or appreciating the beauty that nature offers you.
- Spend time in meditation or prayer, and build yourself up with positive affirmations.
- Pay attention to any signs that your spiritual guides may be leaving for you.
- It is never a good idea to lie to anyone, especially yourself; always be honest with yourself.
- Make a list of everything important to you, and that adds value to your life.
- Be patient with yourself.

Identifying Communication Channels

Communication is an important aspect of our lives. Everyone—from humans to animals—communicates. I chose to focus the attention on listening, because I do believe that it is one of the most important methods of communication. I believe that we are all guilty of hearing what we want, and dismissing the message being conveyed. How do you expect to grow your spiritual universe if you can't, or won't, listen to your spiritual guides? I would like to share a couple of communication channels that can be paired with listening. You may or may not be surprised to know that listening is the life and soul of all forms of communication. It is just a case of applying the tool, splashing on some oil, and making everything work like a well-oiled machine.

The Art of Using Your Voice

You don't have to be a musician to have your voice heard. You don't need any special talents to have your voice heard. You may have missed some of my messages where I told you that you are special. You were given many gifts on the day you entered this world. One of those gifts was using your voice. You ensured that everyone within your radius could hear you. You were never afraid to use your voice. What changed between then and now? Why did you apply a silencer to your voice? Why did you stop using your voice? It is time to remove that silencer. You are going to use your voice to get others to listen. You are going to learn to listen to yourself. Use your voice to scream, talk, and sing. Kick fear out the door, and fill your spiritual universe with fearless voices.

Sharing Is Not All About One Person

Communication is not all about having a voice, or listening to what someone is trying to say. I have found that people are competitive. They are constantly in need of confirmation or attention. I cannot speak for other people, and it may be speculation on my side—but I have noticed a trend where people don't give others the space to share their voices. I am a pretty observant person, and I take note of what is going on around me. I don't make a habit out of eavesdropping on conversations, but it is pretty hard to ignore when people raise their volume a touch higher than normal. One of these raised voice conversations happened at the local grocery store. I suspect it was two friends, as both had carts, and the one was telling the other something. The friend was constantly chiming in with the words; "me," "my," and "I." The other person stopped talking and nodded through the rest of the conversation. It made me realize that we don't want to give others a chance to share what they are going through. We have placed ourselves on a pedestal above others. Sharing should be a two-sided practice. Your spiritual guides want to share their voice with you so that you can share with others.

Communication Channels Are All Around You

Communicating with someone is not only limited to phone calls, Facetiming, instant messaging, writing letters, or singing. You just have to pay close attention to the people around you at the mall, the grocery stores, or on TV. Everything you do is a means of communication. Most often the signs are so tiny that you won't notice them. It is one of those instances that, when it is pointed out, you can't ignore it. Let me show you a few examples before we move on to the next section of our journey. Communication channels are found in:

- the way you walk
- the way you sway your hips
- the way you interact with someone
- the way you tilt your head when talking to someone
- the way you twirl your hair
- the way you dance
- the way you smile
- the way you frown
- the way you cry

The list is never-ending, and now it is up to you to clear the barrier that has prevented you from practicing your communication skills. Remember, it's not all about *you* all the time.

Tapping Into Different Spiritual Practices

Everything that has been discussed in this chapter has been echoed by various spiritual practitioners. The main takeaway is that everyone has a voice that needs to be heard and respected. The fifth spiritual energy is about removing the soundproofing that prevents you from using your communication skills effectively. You know that you can use your voice to be heard, as well as to allow someone else to use theirs. It is not a competition to see who can speak the most, stay silent the longest, or use their voices for no good. Remember to use your tools to keep your spiritual universe happy at all times.

Sound in Color

What would you choose if you were told to decide which color best describes sound? If you have been around since the beginning of the book, you will know that anything goes, and that all answers are right. I would have chosen a mixture of tie-dye colors to represent sound because of what we have learned in this chapter. Sound is versatile, and it can be paired with anything and still be stunning. This is where I put my opinion in my back pocket and take a step to the side to see what the spiritual practitioners have to say.

It is believed that blue is the color that is associated with sound. The color blue would normally be associated with the blue waters of the ocean, which in turn is linked to peaceful energy. Spiritualists believe that the color blue has a calming effect on people who find themselves in stressful positions, or are diagnosed with anxiety. Instead of looking at the energy of water for the soothing our souls need, our spiritual universe has chosen the color blue for the energy of sound. I do believe that the spiritualist practitioners have once again proven that they know what they are doing

Sound Energy in Hinduism and Buddhism

The last leg of this chapter is the usual visit of Hindu and Buddhist practitioners. We started this journey at the base of the spine, and have steadily made our way up through the zones. The sound energy zone is situated right above where your love energy zone is. This sound energy zone is strategically placed, so that you can use your communicative channels with love and affection. I would love to think of the sound energy zone as being the filter before saying something to cause the other person harm, as well as allowing you to listen to what is being said.

Chapter 8:

Enlightenment: Using the Light of Your Spiritual Universe to Awaken What's Been Hidden

The sixth leg of the journey through your spiritual universe is something that affects everyone. I have previously mentioned that we go through life on autopilot. It is easier to believe what others are saying, because they are the ones who are supposed to be knowledgeable. I think about educators who are shaping the minds of their students. Most are afraid to challenge those who have degrees in their field of expertise.

I would like you to think back to when you were younger. Reach out to your family or caregivers to refresh your memory if you need a refresher. I believe that you may have been very creative when you were growing up. You would spend hours coloring, or practicing some form of arts and crafts. You may have raided your parents' closet and played dress-up. You may even have had an imaginary friend who got you into trouble more times than you care to remember.

You buried your imagination, your carefree nature, and your curiosity as you grew up. Your memories gathered more dust as each year passed. The dust from the archives has hidden the memories, and has also hidden the feelings of peace and happiness your soul once knew and loved. You were never allowed to retrieve your possessions from the archives, because you were conditioned to forget about them. I will be the first to admit that this has been one of the best spring-cleaning experiences I have ever experienced or had the privilege to participate in.

Many spiritualists believe that the sixth energy on our spiritual road map is the window to your soul. We are going to perform some magical hocus-pocus—just the normal cleaning techniques—to clear away the many layers of dust that have obscured your outlook on life. It is time to free your imagination and share your story with those around you. Who knows, your story may be the one that will help someone understand the turmoil they are experiencing.

Allow Your Light to Shine

I have found that people are afraid to stand out. No one wants to risk being pointed at, gossiped about, or made fun of because they may see and perceive things differently. You will find some brave souls that are not bothered by the commentary, but many are intimidated. It is part of our human nature to want to protect ourselves from being hurt. I previously mentioned that people are braver when hiding behind their devices, because this gives them the courage to say what they really believe to be true. I have always thought of this as being a bit cowardly in some instances. Some may agree that it is cowardly, and others may say that it is a clever strategic practice to allow others to think about their options.

You and I form part of the seven billion people that inhabit this earth. We know that it is impossible to place everyone into structured categories. We also know that we cannot please everyone. It is up to each of us, as individuals, to share our special gifts with those who we encounter along our journey through life. It is time to come out of hiding; no more hiding away behind others or devices. This journey has taught you to be who you want to be without fear. Each one of us is stronger than those who take pleasure in running others down with their comments. We may not succeed in stopping the spread of hateful, judgmental, or vindictive comments; but nothing prevents us from smothering them in kindness.

You are going to continue planting your seeds of life and light to show others that their negativity does not affect you. You are not going to react to the negativity coming from others. You are going to wash the grimy windows, and clear the cobwebs that have obscured your vision. The hidden windows to your soul will be sparkling with the renewed vision that you last had when you were a young child. What are you waiting for? Come one, grab your bucket filled with positivity and your cloth of clarity, and let's get cleaning.

Tried and Tested Cleaning Methods and Tools

We have ascertained that people are afraid to step outside of their comfort zones. I do find it troubling that some people may find it necessary to step on or crush the dreams, hopes, and aspirations of friends, family, or strangers. I believe that the key takeaway of this book is to prove to you that you have the power to make decisions for yourself. All the books I have written, and those I'm intending to write in the future, will follow a similar narrative. I am giving you a personalized platform that is tailor-made for you. The beauty of having a personalized platform is that you have the freedom to add, remove, or move around whatever you want to fit in with your lifestyle.

I am the interior decorator of your spiritual universe. I give you many suggestions that may or may not work in your spiritual universe. At no point are you forced to do anything that you aren't comfortable doing. The suggestions you are presented with are interchangeable and can be used or amended to work for you. This virtual journey through your spiritual universe doesn't require you to have a fixed address, nor does it require banking information. Your religious or spiritual practices will not count for or against you.

Diet

I bet you were wondering when the topic of what you consume would pop up. This is the only time I will be telling you that you need to put all your candy, chips, crackers, and cookies in a box, wrap it up, and send it to me. You know, that "out of sight, out of mind" game we love to do with our human or fur children. Oh, I'm only kidding, but I also bet you knew that! No one is going to tell you that you need to stop eating the Cadbury mini eggs, or that you should probably stop running to Taco Bell for lunch every second day. You may be cautioned to take care of your body a little better, and make healthier options. Please remember that the mention of diet in this instance has got nothing to do with weight. This is all about giving you some ideas to help you hone in on your spiritual energy that has been lost or dormant.

Spiritualists have said that a nutritious diet will help clear the grime that is blocking the window to your soul. I do believe that the spiritualists have a valid point in their assessment. How can your mind operate at full capacity if your body is feeling sluggish? I found an article written by Leigh Weingus for an online publication, Well+Good. Weingus references a yoga instructor and specialist by the name of Claire Grieve who shares her advice. The advice given is that you are going to have to start focusing on what you are consuming if you want to enjoy spiritual clarity and freedom. Grieve suggests a diet that contains purple foods will help with the enlightenment energy in your spiritual universe. What kind of purple foods would you be looking for at the store? Grieve gives a sample list of foods that you can include in your shopping list, and these are: eggplants, purple cabbage, blackberries, purple kale, acai berries, and passion fruit (Weingus, 2021).

Utilizing Essential Oils

There is nothing more relaxing than walking into a room that instantly puts you at ease. You are embraced by a sense of peace and calm. I spoke to an elderly lady who shared a story about the day she was introduced to essential oils. She told me that the closest she had ever been to essential oils was when her favorite perfumes were oil-based. The perfumes that she had were never used to make the house smell nice—that is what room sprays and air fresheners were used for. She fondly remembers the transition from sprays to wall-plug scents. The first time she saw a diffuser was when her granddaughter gave her one as a gift. She believes that the diffuser, along with the oils she purchases every month, helps keep her calm and brings peace into her home.

Yes, this lady is right in that the oils you use fill your house with positive energy. Everyone has their favorite scents, and it all boils down to personal choice. Some people love the smell of lavender, others like sandalwood, and then you have the adventurous who like to mix things up by mixing jasmine and vanilla. The sky's the limit, and if you are using essential oils, the chances are that the window to your soul is already being worked on. This, again, is not a reflection of negativity if you cannot bear to have smells in your living area. Not everyone can handle smells. This is a perfect example to prove that not everyone's the same.

Breathing and Meditation

I chose to group these two activities together because I believe that they are similar in what they bring to the game. We know that the purpose of this chapter is to give you clarity and freedom from being put in a box. This entire chapter has been about showing you how to rearrange and redecorate your spiritual universe to accommodate you and your needs. This is your journey, and I am along for the ride.

We know that breathing is important to our existence. If we cease to breathe, we become one with nature, and we are no longer part of the living. Many of the alternative spiritual practices place a lot of emphasis on focusing on breathing. It is believed that regulated breathing helps to keep you grounded. It is an excellent tool to bring peace to your soul and soothe your anxiety.

Breathing techniques are often the glue that brings many practices together, such as yoga and meditation. I have spoken to many people who struggle with severe anxiety disorders, and even with the help of medication, they need to practice their breathing techniques. One gentleman told me how he found breathing and meditation to help him when his anxiety crippled him multiple times a day. His doctor had been observing him at one of his health checks and had seen an anxiety attack begin. The doctor stood before him and led him in a guided meditation. The first step was to get him to regulate his breathing by focusing on the ceiling fan above him. When his breathing was in rhythm with the fan, his heart rate had slowed down.

The doctor then had the gentleman lying on the bed and guided him through meditation. The gentleman was not a believer in meditation, because he believed that it went against his beliefs—but he now remembers leaving the doctor's rooms feeling at peace with himself. The whole experience, from the beginning stages of the anxiety to disabling a full-blown attack, took 45 minutes. He is no longer a regular visitor to the doctor's rooms, because he has learned to master the art of meditation and breathing to keep him grounded. He also attributes his new practices to giving him a clearer vision of where he is in his life journey. He did mention that he would be starting yoga so that he could learn to align his spiritual universe.

Tapping Into Different Spiritual Practices

Each leg of this journey through your spiritual universe has brought you closer to the bright shining light. You have learned many lessons on this journey. You have added tricks and tips to your tool belt. You have gained a universe full of knowledge and understanding. The light at the end of this tunnel is shining a little brighter because you have a better view of what the world around you looks like. You are finally starting to believe that you don't need to hide who you are. You don't have to justify yourself to anyone. The shadows are becoming nonexistent, because you have worked hard at clearing away any obstacles that interfere with your spiritual growth.

I know you were skeptical when you started on this journey. It took a lot of convincing to get you to where you are now. You have finally started accepting yourself. You may not see it in yourself, but you have grown along this journey. If you have made it this far into the book, and you are still reading, then you are here for a reason. Something in this book resonates with your feelings. I believe that everything happens for a reason. You don't have to belong to a specific religion, nor do you have to believe in a specific spiritual practice, to understand your feelings.

At the beginning of this chapter, I mentioned that spiritualists believe that the sixth spiritual energy may be associated with the windows of your soul. Everything I have mentioned in this chapter has pointed toward light-related observations. Every stop along this journey has been building up to where we are now. You are standing in front of the windows of your soul. You are looking out at the scenery in front of you. You have a choice to make regarding what you are seeing before you. Remember, life is full of choices. You get to make a choice that you feel is right for you. You may encounter a couple of wrong turns before you get to the right one, but it is all about your outlook on life.

Everyone has a choice. I have mentioned it multiple times, so that you know your rights as a levelheaded, clear-thinking person. You have worked extremely hard to clear the railway line through your spiritual universe. You deserve to reap the rewards you have uncovered and unclogged along the way. I love the spiritual energy of enlightenment. It allows your imagination to come out of hiding, it gives you a clear vision of what you are attempting to achieve, and it helps you see what the naked eye cannot see. The spiritual energy of enlightenment, if taken care of as previously mentioned, will protect you from yourself during times when your vision becomes blurry.

Enlightenment in Color

I am going to miss playing the color game when this book comes to an end. Each of my guesses have been wrong, and instead of frustrating me, it has opened up a new world for me. You aren't the only one learning new things on this journey. I am continually adding bits and pieces to my carry-on luggage that I never knew about. As the writer, I have to read through everything multiple times, and with each read-through, I pick up something new. As for the color guessing game, I have given up because I know that my guesses are way off. If someone were to ask me what color I would associate with light or enlightenment, I would have said, without thinking twice—white. Wouldn't you know it, I got it wrong again.

Spiritualists believe that the color indigo represents the spiritual energy of enlightenment. You have learned why and how you should take care of your spiritual universe. You have been given the freedom and confidence to express your thoughts. You have learned that it is okay to awaken your imagination and follow the dreams you have been hiding. You have even learned that you can share your spiritual wisdom at appropriate times without overwhelming your receivers. Spiritualist practitioners add a warning to the color indigo, and this acts as a reminder to all spiritual adventurists to use the tools prescribed in this chapter to maintain a healthy area around your spiritual energy of enlightenment.

Enlightenment in Hinduism and Buddhism

The last leg of this chapter sees us stopping in for a visit to the Hindu and Buddhist practitioners. The second to last zone on the journey through your spiritual universe takes you to the topic of discussion throughout this chapter. You have learned, throughout your spiritual journey, that each spiritual practice has its own name for descriptive purposes. The Hindus and Buddhists are no different, and they have given the spiritual energy of enlightenment a unique placement and description. The sixth energy zone is believed to be located in the middle of the forehead, in the space between your eyes. They call this area the "third eye," which—when you take a step back and think about it—is the summary of everything that has been mentioned in this chapter.

Are you a mom, dad, or caregiver? Have you ever told your children that you have eyes at the back of your head? Well, here is all the proof you ever needed. You do have a third eye. Don't forget to take care of your newly uncovered spiritual gift.

Chapter 9:

Mind: Integrating the Line of Communication That Speaks Directly to Your Spiritual Universe

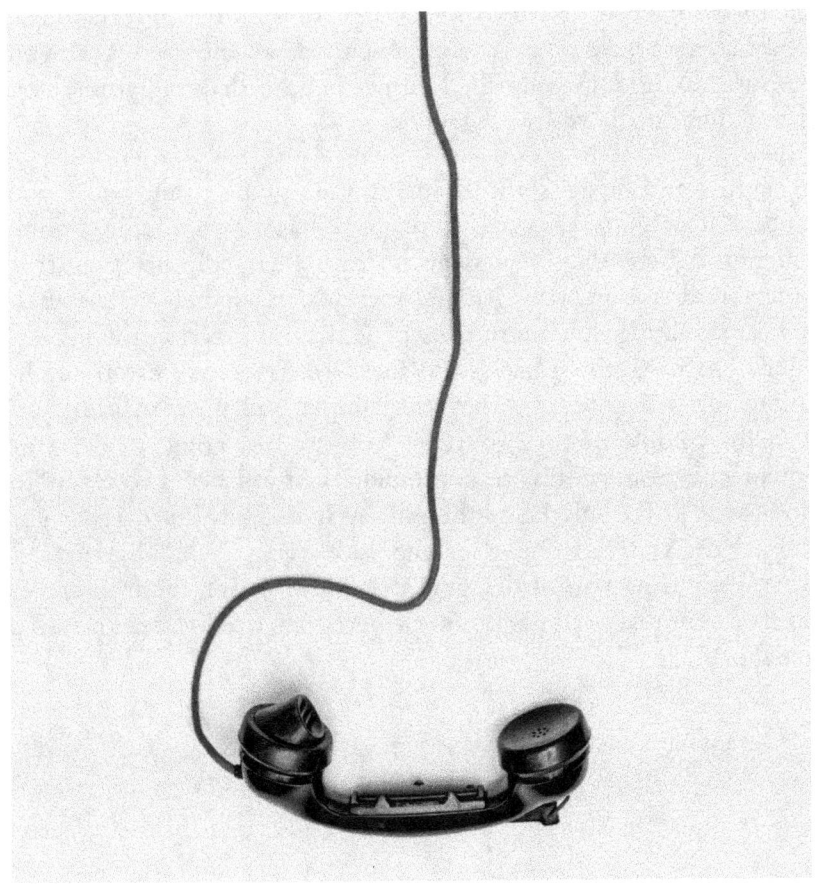

Welcome to the seventh, and final, stop of the journey through your spiritual universe. This is the part of the journey where you get to assemble all the pieces of the puzzle. You learned many things during this journey of self-discovery. You have a clearer understanding of what is going on in your spiritual universe. The tips, tricks, and tools that you have acquired along the way have helped teach you that you are important to yourself and others. I do believe that I have succeeded in proving to you that you are worthy of respect, self-love, and the freedom to make decisions for yourself.

This journey was not as easy as you first thought it would be. You may have expected to read this book to learn about the spiritual energies, and find ways to poke holes in what you have read. Instead, you discovered that your choices were taken into consideration at all times. You learned that you weren't judged, bullied, or condemned. You also learned to embrace your curiosity about your spiritual universe. The part you may not have enjoyed very much was all the hard work you had to put into finding yourself. I firmly believe that everything you have learned has made you stronger.

The seventh—and final—spiritual energy I am going to introduce you to is special. Everyone has gone through a phase (or a couple) during their lifetime where they veered away from their spirituality and/or their religion. I like to call them distractions. Each person has their reasons for doubting their spirituality or faith, and it is not my place—nor yours—to force them back onto the path. Everyone has the right to explore other avenues, or they can simply pull up a rock and sit down in the middle of their journey. You are not going to delay or prevent anyone from starting or continuing their journey if you were to pull up a tock in the middle of the railway line. Your journey has got nothing to do with anyone else, and vice versa. What happens if someone is accusing you of dragging them down? Tell them to take a look at their spiritual road map to see where they need to return to for maintenance.

Setting up the Line of Communication

Did you know that I could easily have skipped Chapters 4 to 9? This train ride we have embarked on could have gone directly from the center of your spiritual universe to your thought palace. What fun is it to go on a one-way trip, though? Maybe it is a means to get to your destination sooner. Maybe it is because of laziness? Maybe it is because you are afraid to be adventurous. I had nothing to do with setting up this journey. I am one of the tools you picked up on your journey of self-discovery. I joined this journey as a member of your support team; the one that shares stories and offers support when encouragement is necessary.

This book has been about connecting all the pieces of your spiritual universe. You had to visit each of the seven stops to clear them out, and fix the blockages. Every process and stop along this journey has been a necessity. It had to happen in the order it did to ensure you didn't skip through any of the steps. It was designed in such a way, so as to lead you to the ultimate prize. Everything that has happened on this journey through your spiritual universe was foreseen long before you thought of it.

Your deity—whether it is God, Allah, Mother God, Mother Nature, or Buddha—was prepared for the day you would start asking questions, wanted to change religions or beliefs, or simply needed to find yourself. It has been said multiple times, and I will continue reiterating it; you have choices. I know and understand the difficulty in keeping others out of your mind palace, but you hold the keys and the cards to restrict entry. Don't ever be afraid to lock someone out. The days of saying, "Yes dear," "No dear," "I will dear," or "I will drop everything right now dear," are over. Everyone should feel at peace in having their voices heard over the rising panic that the global population has created. No more hiding behind the barricades of fear, judgment, or condemnation.

Opening the Doors to Your Mind Palace

I want to remind you that you haven't gone through the process of discovering hidden gems in your spiritual universe to sit back and observe. No friend, it is time to step up to the podium, and show everyone how your spiritual energies shine through you. Let's get to work on cleaning up the last energy on your route. You are going to pick away the stickers that have been hiding your mind palace. Remember to continue using the tools you have acquired since the beginning of this journey.

Opening the doors to your mind palace will present you with many different options to improve yourself and your lifestyle. This is the place where you will retreat to when you need to be alone with your thoughts, and is also the place where you will always find safety and be safe. It is here that you will have a direct line of communication with your spiritual guide or deities. You don't need the newest smartphone on the market or the fastest Internet connection to utilize this amazing facility. All that you need is to love yourself, be truthful to yourself, be kind to yourself, and respect yourself. I have complete faith that you will tick off all the boxes to achieve the maximum results to keep your spiritual universe working.

However (I bet you saw this coming), I want to let you know that you will have to work hard to keep your mind palace clean and free of clutter. It is not a reflection on you, as a person; but it is something that happens in real life, as well as in our spiritual lives. We try to live a minimalist lifestyle, but along the way, you unintentionally collect bits and pieces. Before you know where you are, you are staring at a closet or a cabinet that is bursting at the seams with items you don't need, have grown out of, or just collected for the fun of it. Absolutely no judgment coming from me, and neither should it come from anyone else, because this is something everyone is guilty of.

Knowing When You Have Too Much Clutter

I have often heard people say that they are like sponges who soak up all residual feelings and energies. It is part of our genetic makeup to want to help everyone with their problems. We tend to forget that we are not Atlas, who can carry the world on his shoulders. What happens when you have too much food on your plate? Do you force yourself to eat everything, or do you push the plate away once you have had enough? I believe you may push the plate away, be polite about it, and ask for a takeaway that you can eat the next day.

I have heard of situations where people are forced to eat everything that is on their plates. These are done by people who want to see you fail. Forcing you to do something against your will is a means to gain control of your mind palace. This is where the cracks start appearing, and you will move things around to block the other person's way in. What you end up doing is disconnecting yourself from your direct connection with your deity, because you are protecting yourself. You don't have to move anything around to stand up to those who don't respect you. Use your direct line and ask for help. Use what you learned in Chapter 7 to fine-tune your listening skills and strengthen your communication channels.

Spiritualists believe that one can easily become overwhelmed when your mind palace is in disarray or full of clutter. You can become confused, anxious, and lazy because you have lost the desire to clear the way. I know that it is difficult to keep a home neat and pristine every second of every day. This is why a thorough cleaning is recommended as often as possible, in order to avoid the stresses that come with having too much clutter. Don't be afraid to get rid of containers that don't have lids, or socks that lost their partners to the Bermuda Triangle—better known as the washing machine and dryer. What goes on in your spiritual universe is based on the real-life story of what is going on in your world. It may be in your nature to want to help everyone that crosses your path, but always remember that you are only human. You are in control, and only you can coordinate what goes on in your mind palace. It's better to be exhausted for one day, than to struggle with a case of chronic lackluster.

Guilt-Free Tips and Confidence-Boosting Tips to Clearing Clutter

I believe that this should be a course offered to everyone. I have witnessed people struggling with the task of letting go of physical possessions. They don't care that a mug they used when they were children has a crack. They don't care whether their favorite Danielle Steel book is falling apart. All they care about is that they have memories that may disappear when the items have been removed. I would like to reassure you that memories are stored in your heart. No one can ever take away your memories, unless you decide to discard them.

I had someone share an experience with me that I had to use. They were hoarders, and refused to part with any of their late mother's possessions. They kept old clothes because maybe someone else in the family would like them. They kept plastic containers that were older than they were. They even had old magazines and newspapers dating back to the 1980s because someone may need them for school projects. Someone sat them down and asked them a few questions which they had to think about:

- What is going to happen when you have reached the end of your time on this earth?
- What are you going to do with all the stuff you are keeping?

- Are you going to make a provision in your last will and testament that you will require two coffins?

The point of this exercise was to show them that they were holding onto physical items. These items had sentimental value to them, and not to anyone else. They were told that the memories attached to the items were locked in their souls, and they would be there for all eternity. The way you entered this world, with nothing, is the way you will leave it. They said that they decided to clear out the clutter by donating and selling items they would not use. The money they received from all sales was donated to a charity of choice.

Other helpful decluttering tools include practicing yoga, meditation, and following a nutritious diet. I have also heard people talk about spending time in prayer and worship. Others have mentioned that they dedicate one day a week to volunteering at local charities to help them appreciate what they have. The whole idea of creating a direct line between your mind palace and your deity is for you to learn how to see, and appreciate, what is around you. If you are going to keep the line of communication free of clutter, then you can also enjoy the perks of this clutter-free mind palace I've been referring to. The perks include being motivated, having a good night's rest, being at peace with your choice, and appreciating yourself for the person you have become along this journey.

Tapping Into Different Spiritual Practices

The light at the end of the tunnel is shining brightly. You are moments away from stepping out into the real world. Would you agree with me that the last leg of our journey has been interesting? I use the word *interesting* because it is preparing you for the world beyond your spiritual universe. I know that you may be preparing an argument about why you need to remain in your spiritual universe. I also know that you are afraid of leaving your safety net. It is time to remove the training wheels on the bicycle, to let go of your baby's hand, and loosen the reins. You need to learn how to experience life beyond the safety glass.

It may sound harsh, but everyone has to start somewhere. I met someone who had never lived on their own. They had lived with their parent and sibling until the sibling moved to another state. The person who lived with their parent worked away from home. They opted to stay with their parent because their parent was getting on in years. When the parent suddenly passed away, they were suddenly faced with the fear of living alone. It was new to them. The first couple of months were difficult, but they got through it because they had to. They were forced to adjust to their new journey through life. The hardest choices and decisions are the ones that make you stronger. What does all of this have to do with what is going on in your mind palace? I'm so happy that you asked, because it is one of those examples that shows you that you will always be learning to do new things. You will never be too old to try new activities, or embark on difficult adventures. I would like to publicly say that while I love trying new things, I do draw the line at swimming with sharks; and I also will not eat certain parts of animals that are not found at my local grocery store.

The seventh and final leg of this journey has led you through your spiritual universe. You started this journey from the very bottom of your spiritual universe. You were in darkness for most of the way, and the light became brighter the closer you got to the final stop. The bright light shining after the obligatory sprucing up of your zone let you know that all channels of communication between you and your spiritual guide were free of debris. You knew, the moment you saw the light and heard the call, that you were ready to pursue your destiny on this earth. This chapter has been about helping you connect with your spiritual guide, keeping the line of communication clear, and listening to what is being asked of you. Remember to keep your mind palace free of clutter, and to keep an ear out for any spiritual messages.

The Mind in Color

I have developed a fascination for the different colors and what they represent as part of this journey. I would have chosen a rainbow of colors for the spiritual energy of the mind as the last leg of the journey, but I would have been wrong—yet again. I may not have nailed the rainbow of colors, but you are in for a treat. Spiritualists believe that the spiritual energy of the mind is represented by two different colors.

This is the first time since we embarked on this journey that we have had two colors, which makes it exciting. The colors that spiritualists have pointed out are purple and white. They are standalone colors, and each represents something unique—yet they embrace the meaning behind the spiritual energy of the mind.

The color purple is believed to represent gifts that are true to your spiritual nature. It is easy to get lost in the maze we create in our minds when we are forced to break tradition or step out of our comfort zone. The color purple is a reminder that you are a strong, energetic, humble, honest, bubbly, passionate, and tender-hearted human being. I do believe that these are some of the most beautiful traits for everyone to have. That is why it is important to keep your mind palace free of clutter. I previously mentioned that it is good practice to do a deep clean once in a while to keep the energy flowing freely.

The color white is believed to represent your perfection in the eyes of your spiritual guide. You were created in the image of the Creator, and in their eyes, you have no flaws. Everything, from the hair on your head to the sixth toe on your foot, is as it should be. Everyone was created for a purpose and destined to be part of something that has yet to be revealed. I like to believe that white is the color of a blank canvas that still needs to be created with the help of your spiritual guide.

The Mind in Hinduism and Buddhism

The very last leg of this chapter and the journey through your spiritual universe ends with a visit to our favorite Hindu and Buddhist practitioners. The seventh energy zone is believed to be located at the top of the head, which some may say is the brain. The Hindus and Buddhists refer to the seventh energy zone as the crown. Everything that has been unpacked and mentioned in this chapter has prepared you for this final revelation of what to expect from your spiritual energy of the mind. You have been cautioned multiple times throughout this chapter that you would need to work at keeping this precious energy zone clean. Everyone knows that it is very easy to soak up the grease and dust, which equates to negativity and causes blockages. Use the tools you have been given since you started your journey, and keep your mind energy zone clean.

Conclusion

Can you believe that we have reached the end of the journey through your spiritual universe? My vision, when I started this book, was to create a safe space for everyone who wanted to learn more about their spirituality. I wanted this space to be free of all derogatory and negative energy. I do believe that I have created a safe zone to suit everyone's lifestyle. I have stipulated many times that it doesn't matter where you are in your religious or spiritual maze. It doesn't matter which spiritual practices you follow. All that matters is that you have found a place that offers you an all-inclusive, one-stop approach to be who you want. It is not about the choices you make. It is not about who and what you believe in. It is about who you are, and where you want to go on your journey through life.

Graduation Time

You are about to graduate from *Spiritual Energies: Awaken What's Within You With Everything You Need to Know About the 7 Spiritual Energies*, with a doctorate that permits you to live your life to the fullest. Most people would read this, roll their eyes, and say, "Yeah, and?" No one will ever understand the amount of courage that it took you to dig around in your spiritual universe. I know that you were looking over your shoulder multiple times during the first couple of stops. You were waiting for someone to pull you out; or you were waiting for that threat of a lightning bolt striking you down. I also know that you started relaxing around the fourth leg of the journey, where you discovered that you didn't have to be afraid.

Slow and Steady

How would you have led the expedition through your spiritual universe had you been in charge? I can't help but wonder how someone with 'experience' would have conducted this journey. I realize that this is a subject that has many different approaches, and as people normally are, everyone will have an opinion. You may have been frustrated with my approach. I may have taken a little longer to reach the point I was trying to get across. I will ask you again, how would you have led the expedition if you were in charge? I believe that if you were in charge of this journey, you would have rushed from point A to Z to prove that nothing that was discussed had an effect on you. The slow and steady approach is an important one where you have to think. This wasn't a race to see who would reach the end first; it was about finding yourself. The slow and steady approach helped you find yourself behind the barriers, in the caves, under piles of dust, and behind grimy windows. You learned something at every step of this journey. You worked hard to clear away the blockages of fear, judgment, intimidations, and condemnation.

The Journey Ends Here

Your spiritual universe is not meant to be a place that harbors the physical pain of the world around us. This book, and all the others I have written and will write, is about you embracing your imperfections. You need to make peace with yourself, and this book is a reminder that you are not—and never will be—alone. This journey that is reaching its end has something that many are lacking, and that is a spiritual map that was revealed to you—one stop at a time—until the very end. You knew, when you started, that this journey would have seven stops. Each stop was at a zone that would teach you more about yourself. And, at the very end of the journey, as the train pulls into the station where you will disembark, each stop and zone are united to represent seven spiritual energies that have been awakened within you.

References

Baron-Reid, C. (2020, August 3). T*elling a new story - Oracle of the 7 energies!.* Colette Baron-Reid. https://www.colettebaronreid.com/2020/08/03/telling-a-new-story-oracle-of-the-7-energies

Baron-Reid, C. (2021). *Open to the universe by integrating your 7 energies!.* Colette Baron-Reid. https://www.colettebaronreid.com/2021/04/19/what-are-the-seven-energies

Baron-Reid, C. (2022). *6 Tools for spiritual alignment.* Colette Baron-Reid. https://www.colettebaronreid.com/2022/02/01/6-tools-for-spiritual-alignment

Becker, J. (n.d.). *A beginner's guide to exploring spirituality.* Becoming Minimalist. https://www.becomingminimalist.com/exploring-spirituality

Bhimji, S. (2016). *Method and rulings of wudhu'.* Al-Islam.org. https://www.al-islam.org/articles/method-and-rulings-wudhu-saleem-bhimji

Bible Gateway. *1 John 3:16-18 NIV.* (n.d.). BibleGateway.com. https://www.biblegateway.com/passage/?search=1+John+3%3A16-18&version=NIV

Brian, P. (2021, June 2). *How to listen to your soul: 10 Steps to discover what you really want.* Nomadrs. https://nomadrs.com/how-to-listen-to-your-soul

Building Beautiful Souls. (n.d.-a). *Element of Earth symbolism and meaning.* BuildingBeautifulSouls.com. https://www.buildingbeautifulsouls.com/symbols-meanings/five-elements-symbolic-meaning/element-earth

Building Beautiful Souls. (n.d.-b). *Element of fire symbolism and meaning.* BuildingBeautifulSouls.com. https://www.buildingbeautifulsouls.com/symbols-meanings/five-elements-symbolic-meaning/fire-element-symbolic-meaning

Building Beautiful Souls. (n.d.-c). *Element of water symbolism and meaning.* BuildingBeautifulSouls.com. https://www.buildingbeautifulsouls.com/symbols-meanings/five-elements-symbolic-meaning/element-water

Building Beautiful Souls. (n.d.-d). *Solar plexus chakra (manipura chakra): Healing, meditation, meaning, stones & crystals.* BuildingBeautifulSouls.com. https://www.buildingbeautifulsouls.com/symbols-meanings/chakra-colors-chakra-symbols/solar-plexus-chakra-meaning-healing

Building Beautiful Souls. (n.d.-e). *What does the color blue mean.* BuildingBeautifulSouls.com. https://www.buildingbeautifulsouls.com/symbols-meanings/color-psychology-symbolism-meanings/what-does-the-color-blue-mean

Building Beautiful Souls. (n.d.-f). *What does the color green mean.* BuildingBeautifulSouls.com. https://www.buildingbeautifulsouls.com/symbols-meanings/color-psychology-symbolism-meanings/what-does-the-color-green-mean

Building Beautiful Souls. (n.d.-g). *What does the color indigo mean.* BuildingBeautifulSouls.com. https://www.buildingbeautifulsouls.com/symbols-meanings/color-psychology-symbolism-meanings/what-does-the-color-indigo-mean

Building Beautiful Souls. (n.d.-h). *What does the color purple mean.* BuildingBeautifulSouls.com. https://www.buildingbeautifulsouls.com/symbols-meanings/color-psychology-symbolism-meanings/what-does-the-color-purple-mean

Building Beautiful Souls. (n.d.-i). *What does the color white mean.* BuildingBeautifulSouls.com. https://www.buildingbeautifulsouls.com/symbols-meanings/color-psychology-symbolism-meanings/what-does-the-color-white-mean

Building Beautiful Souls. (n.d.-j). *What does the color yellow mean.* BuildingBeautifulSouls.com. https://www.buildingbeautifulsouls.com/symbols-meanings/color-psychology-symbolism-meanings/what-does-the-color-yellow-mean

Cameron, Y. (2021, October 29). *A beginner's guide to the 7 chakras + how to unblock them.* Mindbodygreen. https://www.mindbodygreen.com/0-91/The-7-Chakras-for-Beginners.html

Chase. (n.d.). *Symbolism of fire: Spiritual, dreams, history.* Firefighter Insider. https://firefighterinsider.com/symbolism-fire-spiritual-dreams

Chow, S. (2021, March 18). *Meditation history.* News-Medical.net. https://www.news-medical.net/health/Meditation-History.aspx

Christopher. (2020, November 24). *Earth Symbolism.* Symbolism & Metaphor. https://symbolismandmetaphor.com/symbolism-of-earth

Das, S. (2019, April 12). *The Ganges: Hinduism's holy river.* Learn Religions. https://www.learnreligions.com/ganga-goddess-of-the-holy-river-1770295

Deibe, I. (2021, April 19). *Third eye meaning: What is the third eye? What happens when you open it?.* Express.co.uk. https://www.express.co.uk/life-style/life/1425264/third-eye-meaning-what-is-the-third-eye-what-happens-when-you-open-it-how-to-unblock-evg

Dowshen, S. (2022, January). *Carbohydrates and diabetes.* KidsHealth.org. https://kidshealth.org/en/teens/carbs-diabetes.html

Estrada, J. (2019, April 22). *10 Tips to align your mind, body, and spirit when regular life blows up your balance.* Well+Good. https://www.wellandgood.com/mind-body-and-spirit

Goodreads. (n.d.-a) *A quote by Benjamin Franklin.* Goodreads.com. https://www.goodreads.com/quotes/340402-don-t-put-off-until-tomorrow-what-you-can-do-today

Goodreads. (n.d.-b). *If you see me talking to myself just move along I'm self employed and having a staff meeting.* Goodreads.com. https://www.goodreads.com/book/show/49134547-if-you-see-me-talking-to-myself-just-move-along-i-m-self-employed-and-ha

Hurst, K. (2017). *How to open your crown chakra - A beginners guide.* The Law Of Attraction. https://www.thelawofattraction.com/crown-chakra-healing

Hyl, T. (2015). *The spiritual meaning of fire.* Tony Hyland Psychic Services. https://www.tonyhyland.com/rw/the-spiritual-meaning-of-fire

Martin, S. (2018). *How to love yourself: 22 Simple ideas.* Live Well with Sharon Martin. https://www.livewellwithsharonmartin.com/how-to-love-yourself

Merriam-Webster. (2019a). *Definition of ENERGY.* Merriam-Webster.com. https://www.merriam-webster.com/dictionary/energy

Merriam-Webster. (2019b). *Definition of LOVE.* Merriam-Webster.com. https://www.merriam-webster.com/dictionary/love

Merriam-Webster. (2019c). *Definition of ORACLE.* Merriam-Webster.com. https://www.merriam-webster.com/dictionary/oracle

Merriam-Webster. (2019d). *Definition of RELIGION.* Merriam-Webster. https://www.merriam-webster.com/dictionary/religion

Miller's Guild. (2022). *10 Spiritual meanings of water.* MillersGuild.com. https://www.millersguild.com/spiritual-meaning-of-water

Mind Fuel Daily. (2014). *Finding your spiritual center.* MindFuelDaily.com. https://www.mindfueldaily.com/livewell/finding-your-spiritual-center

Ness, K. (n.d.). *Heart chakra: Here's everything you need to know about your fourth chakra.* YogiApproved. https://www.yogiapproved.com/the-heart-chakra-how-it-impacts-your-ability-to-love-and-be-loved

Perlman, H. (2019, November 13). *How much water is there on Earth?*. usgs.gov. https://www.usgs.gov/special-topics/water-science-school/science/how-much-water-there-earth

Putnam, R. (n.d.). *What is the spiritual meaning of the color red?*. Crystal Clear Intuition. https://crystalclearintuition.com/spiritual-meaning-of-red

The Quran. (n.d.). *The Quran*. Al-quran.info. https://al-quran.info/#5:6

ReGain. (2022, January 28). *Best & common symbols of love and their meanings*. ReGain.us. https://www.regain.us/advice/general/symbols-of-love-and-their-meanings

Scott, S. (2019, July 8). *Spirituality vs religion: 3 BIG differences between each*. Happier Human. https://www.happierhuman.com/difference-religion-spirituality

Shazi, A. (2021). *The spiritual meaning of water*. Spirituality & Health. https://www.spiritualityhealth.com/spiritual-meaning-of-water

Simonova, L. (2020, March 14). *10 Types of spirituality & spiritual practices to try in 2022*. Happier Human. https://www.happierhuman.com/types-spirituality

TNN. (2019, August 9). *What are the 7 chakras in our body? Here is a complete breakdown*. The Times of India. https://timesofindia.indiatimes.com/life-style/health-fitness/home-remedies/what-are-the-7-chakras-in-our-body-here-is-a-complete-breakdown/articleshow/70605207.cms

Tucker, D., Jr. (2014, June 5). *Remembering God's gift of water*. The Connection. https://sites.duke.edu/theconnection/2014/06/05/remembering-gods-gift-of-water

U.S. Forest Service. (2019). *Fire effects on the environment*. Usda.gov. https://www.fs.usda.gov/pnw/page/fire-effects-environment

Vishnu. (2013). *Who to fall in love with first: 6 Ways to love yourself*. Tiny Buddha. https://tinybuddha.com/blog/who-to-fall-in-love-with-first-6-ways-to-love-yourself

Water and Spirituality. (2013). *Water and spirituality*. HealingEarth. https://healingearth.ijep.net/water/water-and-spirituality

Water Science School. (2019, May 22). *The water in you: Water and the human body*. usgs.gov. https://www.usgs.gov/special-topics/water-science-school/science/water-you-water-and-human-body

Weingus, L. (2021, June 16). *Learning how to open your third eye can help you avoid brain fog—Here are 11 tips to help*. Well+Good. https://www.wellandgood.com/how-to-open-your-third-eye

Wetwetwetmusic. (2013, August 16). *Wet Wet Wet - Love Is All Around (Official Video)* [Video]. YouTube. https://www.youtube.com/watch?v=h3gEkwhdXUE

Wikipedia. (2022, March 3). *Love is all around*. Wikipedia.org. https://en.wikipedia.org/wiki/Love_Is_All_Around

Image References

Andrews, A. (2018, April 17). *Old phone* [Image]. Unsplash. https://unsplash.com/photos/JYGnB9gTCls

Burns, C. (2017, September 10). *Burn it to the ground* [Image]. Unsplash. https://unsplash.com/photos/gyrrWzwqm5Y

Congdon, D. (2021, June 10). *End of the line.* [Image]. Unsplash. https://unsplash.com/photos/hLl5DCBmTnI

Feliciano, L. (2019, November 12). [*HD photo by Luis Feliciano*] [Image]. Unsplash. https://unsplash.com/photos/9EH5AkClwZ0

Gómez, O. (2017, May 14). *Love in the mountains* [Image]. Unsplash. https://unsplash.com/photos/L8-0SAy-aoQ

González, C. (2021, March 15). *Metro of Berlín, Germany* [Image]. Unsplash. https://unsplash.com/photos/bg1--WStcww

Hughes, M. (2018, July 13). *This is the Durbin Rocket, a Heisler No. 6 locomotive - A coal-fired steam engine* [Image]. Unsplash. https://unsplash.com/photos/r5hrXLG_6Ho

Kaethler, K. (2019, February 26). [*Black batteries and eggplant photo*] [Image]. Unsplash. https://unsplash.com/photos/7Pg0qug_D9s

Kaipov, V. (2021, March 8). *DIY workplace. Process: Instagram: @vadimkaipov* [Image]. Unsplash. https://www.instagram.com/p/CMT1Cr-Hy69/ https://unsplash.com/photos/f6jkAE1ZWuY

Kemper, J. (2020, August 19). [*Person holding green plant stem*] [Image]. Unsplash. https://unsplash.com/photos/4z3lnwEvZQw

Meng, Q. (2017, August 4). *Body Grassland in Yili, Xinjiang, China* [Image]. Unsplash. https://unsplash.com/photos/01_igFr7hd4

Palmer, M. (2021, July 6). *A fern grows from ashes after significant bushfires in Tasmania, Australia.* [Image]. Unsplash. https://unsplash.com/photos/qUsVYeuxLIQ

Pechurin, D. (2019, March 17). [*White wooden door photo*] [Image]. Unsplash. https://unsplash.com/photos/JUbjYFvCv00

Prasla, F. (2019, May 24). [*Empty train railroad photo*] [Image]. Unsplash. https://unsplash.com/photos/pClP_yaqQCk

Roller, K. (2017, January 10). [*Person submerged in body of water holding sparkler*] [Image]. Unsplash. https://unsplash.com/photos/PC_lbSSxCZE

Schneiter, B. (2020, June 2). *Golden light on your path* [Image]. Unsplash. https://unsplash.com/photos/r27CD64Qeec

Strulik, T. (2021, September 30). *The famous Skradinski Buk Waterfalls in the Krka National Park. Austria & Croatia roadtrip September 2021* [Image]. Unsplash. https://unsplash.com/photos/pokN6GNRDYg

Tohm, B. (2017, February 18). *Tulips from a lover* [Image]. Unsplash. https://unsplash.com/photos/5lvgkp_xix8

Towner, J. (2016, August 2). *Beam of light on a forest road* [Image]. Unsplash. https://unsplash.com/photos/3Kv48NS4WUU

Yanes, U. (2021, September 5). [*Bread on white ceramic plate beside clear drinking glass*] [Image]. Unsplash. https://unsplash.com/photos/si9efVkuxEo